NAVIGATOR'S LC

NAVIGATOR'S LOG
OF A TOUR IN BOMBER COMMAND

JACK RODGERS

MERLIN BOOKS LTD.
Braunton   Devon

ISBN 0 86303 254-0
Printed in England by Maslands Ltd., Tiverton, Devon

Dedicated
to
W. G. Bickley Esq. CGM
617 Squadron, Bomber Command

CONTENTS

ILLUSTRATIONS

1

1939-40

The origin of this narcissistic chronicle of my experiences in the Royal Air Force sprang from a desire to leave my grandchildren some mental picture of what kind of bloke 'Grandad' was before he left the main runway for the last time. I was particularly unfortunate as a child with my choice of grandparents as one grandad whom I never knew died at an early age of pernicious anaemia in the days when there was no known cure whilst the other lived in the veritable heart of Yorkshire, Leeds, and departed for Elysian Fields when I was the tender age of twelve. However, the latter unwittingly exerted some influence on my life, being one of the earliest incorporated accountants (later chartered) he became company secretary and chief accountant of New Silkstone and Haig Moor Collieries, Castleford. The result was that my father became obsessed with me qualifying as a chartered accountant, an ambition which was destined not to bear fruition although I passed my intermediate exam with comparative ease. My companion when I sat the exam in November 1938 was Jack Pickering, a brilliant inside forward with Sheffield United, later to be capped for England. Jack played his last first division game at the age of forty-two. I look back with pleasure at the luncheons, mostly ploughmans we scoffed, washed down with a pint of Youngers in the popular Westminster bar in Sheffield's High Street. Sad to say, this mecca of the town's business men was destroyed in the blitz.

To recap, I was articled in 1936 to an elderly chartered accountant to whom my father paid a premium of one hundred and fifty pounds, which in those days was equivalent to a working man's annual gross wage — or conversely would have bought a couple of terraced houses. In return, I was paid the princely sum of two shillings and sixpence per week in the first year, rising by equal annual increments to twelve shillings and sixpence in my fifth and final year.

The office personnel consisted of two partners, two typists-cum-clerks, one graduate accountant, two articled clerks and a general manager, George F. M. Airey who was the most distinguished of all as he was a part-time secretary to the brilliant literary lions, the Sitwell family of Renishaw. All this must seem academic but without a doubt, in retrospect, the years of my articles from 1936 to the outbreak of war were happy ones. Life in the office was quite varied, Mondays and Tuesdays I spent collecting rents in the sleazier districts of Sheffield, the tenants had a great sense of humour — they just didn't pay the rent, not if they could help it. One notorious client, I should have said tenant who would have upstaged Gloria Swanson in *Sunset Boulevard* plus twenty years used to shout:

"Come upstairs love, the rent's up here." The fact that I preserved my virginity in this and similar circumstances must be attributed to my sheltered upbringing, as I possessed the same carnivorous desires as any other nineteen-year-old adolescent.

I had very little rapport with my principal as we had an age gap of over fifty years. He very rarely surfaced before lunch and frequently when he disagreed with something I had done or not done in the morning, as the case may be, he would send me home and I would ring up the nearest cricket club playing mid week. The other partner gave me afternoons off for the same purpose, so I had the best of both worlds, not that it advanced my studies that much.

One of the most attractive sides I played for was a University XI called 'The Squirrels' which generally included at least two doctors whose indifference to injuries marked them down as potential pathologists. Later in actual fact, they had distinguished careers and one of them was knighted for his services to medicine.

In the office, we had very few outside jobs with the exception of the biggest store in the east end of the city called Banners, where we used to spend several weeks on audit. This audit was to have a profound effect on my life. It came about because we invariably caught the five-past-five tram back to the city. Trams actually ran to timetables and Sheffield, along with Glasgow, boasted the finest service in the country. Always in the upstairs front bay, colloquially known as the 'greenhouse', was a bevy of typists finding refuge from the shag laden smoke of the steel workers, not very successfully, I might add. One of them stood out in my opinion and since we met every night it was inevitable, despite my retiring manner, that we started chatting and we are still chatting and not chatting to each other after four decades of marital bliss and otherwise.

I used to go on this audit with Kenneth MacDonald who had just qualified, and our triumvirate in the office was completed by Gordon Ebblewhite. We spent many a happy hour discussing cricket and football interspersed by bouts of industry with a view to outwitting the Inland Revenue. Kenneth was eventually commissioned as an accountant officer and our paths crossed once in 1944 when he was a squadron leader and myself a mere flying officer. Gordon who was at least seven years my senior and was 'knocking on' for aircrew nevertheless volunteered as an air gunner. He was shot down in the Mediterranean and qualified as a member of the exclusive 'Goldfish Club'. Unfortunately his luck ran out and he was subsequently killed on operations in the Middle East.

In the winter, I played soccer with Sheffield Club, on record as being the oldest football club in history, and we shared facilities with hockey, squash, Rugby and tennis at Abbeydale Park on the Derbyshire side of Sheffield, a showpiece of sporting facilities. In the Easter prior to the outbreak of hostilities we went on a tour to Hastings and Bexhill. I only took part in one game as I went down with a flu bug and was treated by my cricketing colleague doctors of the aforementioned university side known as the 'Squirrels'. If my memory serves me correct, they coughed up a couple of aspirins between them. The nadir of the tour occurred when some of our party unintentionally barged into the wrong bedroom, modesty forbids me to disclose the status of the occupants. Great days and great companions.

My life revolved around cricket and football and the summer of thirty-nine saw me keeping wicket for Sheffield United, crowning the season by winning the Yorkshire League. The previous year, I was a member of the Mexborough Cricket Club when we won the Yorkshire Council championship. But Bramall Lane was my first love, my family had been associated with Sheffield United both at cricket and football for many years. Myself, two brothers and my father had all at one time or another kept wicket for this famous club. The chairman was Leslie Stubbs who was also on the Yorkshire Committee and I had been given half a promise of a game with Yorkshire Seconds the following season to fulfil an ambition which is indigenous to all fortunate enough to be born within its boundaries.

You may query what this has to do with the war — it has nothing but I have recalled these times to illustrate the extremely happy and uncomplicated circumstances which motivated my life. If I can make a further digression, again about cricket: on one leave, after the war was over, Leslie Stubbs invited me to Bramall Lane to have a look at a new fast bowler they had unearthed. That fast bowler was Fred Trueman.

In the late August, we spent a very pleasant holiday at Clacton on Sea finishing up with a few days in London, but the war clouds loomed ominously. A week after we returned home, the inevitable happened, war was declared and, although I did not realize it, I had played my last game of cricket for ten years.

We spent the first afternoon of the war, which incidentally was a

Sunday, criss-crossing the windows with gummed paper strips and we really thought it was not too soon, as that night the sirens wailed their ghastly warning of the harbingers of death approaching. But it was a false alarm and we returned thankfully, if not a little chastened, into the arms of Morpheus. These alarms continued with fairly monotonous regularity and we wasted many hours with neighbours in an underground cellar.

Aircraft used to come over but danger at that time was minimal and the most likely explanation was the nuisance and loss of production value, whilst at the same time, testing the German beam system known as Knickebein. The Luftwaffe presence was easily recognizable because of the note emitted from the de-synchronized engines.

But now, as far as I was concerned a more mundane fact presented itself, the problem of which service I should honour. I really wasn't disposed to share my talents with any branch of His Majesty's Armed Forces but time and tide wait for no man and since it was inevitable that I would be conscripted, the onus was on me to volunteer. I didn't really fancy the Army having been a private in the school cadet corps which I only joined as a more pleasant alternative to running a five mile cross country in a pair of boots as I had forgotten to take my slippers to school. If any confirmation was required of my non-election for the Army it came near Christmas when my friend and colleague Kenneth MacDonald and myself were engaged on an audit in Hillsborough Barracks, a stone Victorian horror of a place from an aesthetic point of view, but serving as an admirable base for company activities. One lunch-time we went into the main street which was lined with a preponderance of women, several of whom were unashamedly crying. The reason was self-evident when a platoon of territorials came marching down the street. It was poignant as they were obviously destined for France and memories must have flooded back to the First World War when the Sheffield City Battalion was annihilated almost to a man on that never to be forgotten day, July 1st 1916 in the Battle of the Somme.

So the Army was out, I would never have had the guts to stick a bayonet into somebody and I have the most profound admiration for all army types, their conditions and *modus operandi* contrasted starkly with the comfort afforded to us when not operating.

The Royal Navy was never contemplated; living in a land-locked city, any maritime aspirations were out.

At this time I was very friendly with a serving officer, Douglas Parker, a Cambridge soccer blue like his brother and a University Air Squadron pilot. He was flying Hampdens in Bomber Command which together with the Whitley, Wellington and Blenheim were the spearhead of the RAF's offensive in the early days. But the actual damage inflicted on the enemy and his communications in those times was not commensurate with the endeavour expended and the casualties suffered. Aircrew of the calibre of Douglas Parker were a very rare breed.

Operating in the earliest days of the war was a very hazardous business as demonstrated by the loss of five out of eleven Hampdens in September 1939 attacking two destroyers off Heligoland. Because of their daylight vulnerability, they were transferred to night bombing and took part in the first raid on Berlin. Within thirteen months of the outbreak of war two Hampden crew members were awarded the Victoria Cross. The Hampden was a fine aircraft in the best Handley Page tradition and like the Halifax was powered by radial engines. As far as I can gather, one of its main disadvantages was the cramped lay-out which accommodated a crew of four and the facilities for indulging in a 'leak' must have been extremely limited.

Douglas always came on leave to Sheffield and we used to drink in the Prince of Wales at Ecclesall where beer was eight pence a pint (old money). After closing time, we descended on the Grand Hotel, very much the 'in' place in the centre of the city to finish off a convivial evening with coffee and biscuits. What I admired most about him was his temperament; he was ice cold and I would say completely incapable of any kind of flap. Later on when I was in aircrew, I used to look around and wonder — Are they as frightened as I am? But Douglas never talked about what he was doing and never ever shot a line although he must have been one of the first aircrew to be awarded the DFC. Incidentally, at the time of our friendship, I was twenty-two years old and if I wanted to stay out after half-past ten, it was a ritual to ring my mother to obtain her permission — *Tempora mutantur nos et mutamur in illis.* The last occasion I saw Douglas, we had coffee in Daveys in the High Street, another Sheffield landmark. He was then a Flight Lieutenant and I was the lowest of the low, an Aircraftman second class. I never saluted him when parting which was very remiss and much to my regret, I have not seen or heard of him since that morning in 1940.

I suppose our friendship influenced me so I volunteered for the RAF, hoping with my academic qualifications that I could be considered for a commission as an accountant officer. In effect, I was a conscript volunteer, I was bound to be called up so I jumped the gun. My medical took place in the Cutlers' Hall, the bastion of the Master Cutler, the highest honour Sheffield has to offer one of its sons, greatly exceeding the office of Lord Mayor (unless you happen to be the Lord Mayor). I only had three medicals in the whole of my service career and the chief criterion as to the state of your health centred on the MO holding your private parts and saying cough.

Incidentally, I still have the cough. I also remember emphasizing to the doctor that I was completely unwilling to fly.

The next stage was to be attested and I was given a travel warrant to Warrington and the swearing in ceremony was performed with due solemnity on the camp with no Royalty present. Then away to the canteen to imbibe tea heavily laced with bromide. Seeing there were no females available and Warrington is synonymous with Rugby league, this seemed a gross waste of public money.

And so back home to wait the clarion call. Occasionally I kept wicket in charity matches with county cricketers and one game at Millhouses, a suburb of Sheffield stands out. I had stumped three out and whipped off Len Hutton's bails from a leg side delivery, making at the same time a tremendous appeal. A great England and Derbyshire fast bowler, fielding at first slip, turned and reverting to the vernacular said with undisguised disdain — "Tha wants to pack that up — they haven't come to see thee!"

CHAIRBORNE

After waiting several months, the fatal blue paper arrived telling me to report at Blackpool on the 8th October 1940 and bring with me:
1. This paper.
2. Your National Insurance Identity Card and Civilian Ration Book.
3. Your Employment Book and Health and Pensions Insurance Cards.
4. Your Civilian Respirator (Anti-Gas).
5. The RAFVR badge which was issued to you on enlistment.
6. If married, your marriage certificate and birth certificates in respect of children.

I arrived in Blackpool around tea-time and was promptly allotted a billet together with twenty others in a typical seaside boarding-house almost opposite the south pier. There followed all the usual documentation, involving standing around for hours, a state of affairs of which the services seem to have a monopoly. Having satisfied the powers that be that I was the authentic Aircraftman second class, Jack Harold Rodgers, I was photographed and issued with a new identity card. Next came the kitting out and in my case they couldn't find a greatcoat to fit me and I was condemned to march about for the next six weeks in a coat meant for a six footer and I could only make five feet seven standing on tiptoe. It was very humiliating but at least it did something for the morale of the locals and the southern immigrants who adopted Blackpool as a bomb free bolt-hole. There was also the inevitable ritual of sticking needles at random in one's anatomy which included a vaccination session in which one in every half-dozen flaked out.

Most of the days were spent in square bashing which took place in the south shore fun park but it wasn't much joy and as far as I could see developed into a competition between our corporal and the sergeant as to who could shout most. It was quite the longest six weeks in my life and it came as a great relief when my posting as an under training accounts clerk came through and I found myself at the traditional home of the Royal Air Force, Cranwell. Not that we were to see the grandeur that was Rome. We were billeted in what must have been the original quarters, huts with stone

First week in the RAF, 15 October, 1940 — author 1st left, front row

floors and horrible stone sinks in which really hot water was conspicuous by its absence. A central stove disgorging its smoke evenly through the roof and the billet combined with the aroma of drying socks to constitute our home from home.

Being a semi-professional, I found the course comparatively easy but somewhat boring, being very much a form filling effort no doubt devised to minimize the chance of fiddling.

There was certainly less bull but little in the way of entertainment other than dances in a huge but draughty hangar, and as a diversion we frequented neighbouring Sleaford to gorge sausage and chips followed by the latest flick. Whilst I was at Cranwell, two events stand out in my memory. The first when a Luftwaffe plane flew down the intersection of two rows of huts where I was walking, spraying bullets from a height of fifty feet as if they were going out of fashion. It was all over in a matter of seconds and fortunately he sheered off without inflicting damage or casualties. The second was the sight of what I identified as a Handley-Page Heyford, a large, incongruous looking machine which first saw service in 1933 as a heavy night bomber but was seconded to training stations at the beginning of the war of which Cranwell was one. I think this was the time I began to think about flying. I saw two sergeant pilots on the perimeter track, I had always had terrific respect for anyone sporting wings and looking at those brevets I had a great yearning to change places.

After qualifying as a clerk accountant I was posted to 944 Squadron, Grimsby, whose specialist duty was to raise balloons to protect the ports of Grimsby and Hull from low flying aircraft. The work was soul-destroying but the night life amply compensated and we used to drink at the Ship and the Pestle and Mortar before moving on to the sophisticated delights of Cleethorpes, rounding off the evening with a dance on the pier. I formed a friendship with a Corporal Ford who had a successful motor business in Hull. He was older than me and too old to be accepted for flying duties which would have been his metier. We used to tear around in his open MG, a model which is now acknowledged as a classic and it was he who first introduced me to the road. He bought a motor bike in Grimsby and although I had never driven or ridden anything before, I rode it to Hornsea unlicensed, uninsured, and unsafe, across the Grimsby to Hull ferry to the seaside haven where his delightful wife and baby son, whom I nicknamed 'Oppo Minimus', were living. I found I had a great affinity with the feeling of power and speed and although 'Fordy' forbade me to ride it again, I used to sneak out on the open road and fancy myself as a fighter pilot whenever he went out. I was now living in a Walter Mitty world; when I returned to

Grimsby I used to ride a bike like fury down the main street cutting in and out of traffic as though they were enemy aircraft. And so under the influence of Harry Castle, one of the office clerks who had ploughed a pilot's course but could never stop talking about Tiger Moths, I decided to take the plunge.

I was called before a selection board which consisted of four be-gonged officers and subjected to a rigorous oral examination. I passed with flying colours, an apt metaphor, the secret of success being to emphasize a burning desire to fight the enemy; saying that you were brassed off and fed up with being pushed around was hardly a cogent argument. I envisaged being posted immediately to a training unit but instead was shunted off to Aberdeen on another accountancy posting. Circumstances were much more to my liking as my chief, Richard Mansbridge, was a peacetime chartered accountant, and we had much in common. I also used to mix with aircrew from neighbouring Dyce and many a good night we spent in the Douglas, the most popular rendezvous in Aberdeen. But the sombre realities of flying were brought home from time to time when one heard of the casualties on the Station which housed a Polish Squadron. One day a Spit crashed in a field very close to our place of work.

However, in March 1942, two events occurred which were turning points in my life. Firstly, after courting seven years I entered the marital stakes but my betrothed would not have been too happy if she had known that on my way to the nuptials from the banks of the Dee to the murky waters of the Don in Sheffield, a railway porter in the misguided goodness of his heart locked me in a compartment with a Waaf without so much as a 'by your leave'. To say I was literally and metaphorically relieved when we steamed into York without mishap is putting it mildly. And this would have been my stag night in normal circumstances. Our wedding was typical of the wartime austerity vintage enriched however by my best man who sported a kilt as befitted a warrior in a Highland regiment. He was later to be awarded the Military Cross for his exploits as a French Resistance Leader. A few idyllic days marred only by a contretempts with a bull were spent in the Rutland Arms in Bakewell, a hostelry made famous by Jane Austen who spent many pleasant hours here working on *Pride and Prejudice*. It was here also, well over a century ago that saw the origin of the famous 'Bakewell Tart' then known as 'Bakewell Pudding' which was the result of the hotel cook unwittingly reversing a time honoured recipe.

Secondly, flying came a step nearer when I was posted to Number 4 Initial Training Wing at Scarborough where I was billeted in the Grand Hotel, a magnificent edifice which dominated the skyline of the South Bay.

The only time the author was shot down — 21 March, 1942, Sheffield

I had spent many holidays in Scarborough which was almost my second home and here I was again, this time on military service. It was very much akin to joining up as one was again put through the initial routines, but this time it was more exacting. Whereas Blackpool was purely square bashing, here it was more refined and we drilled on the Valley Road and the sea front carrying out marching and counter-marching with variations, making a mental count and not taking orders from the drill sergeant. As I was now a Leading Aircraftman amongst so many rookies I used to be 'joed' for guard commander supposed to be protecting the Grand and the Royal on the opposite side of the square, but it was a thankless job as it involved trying to get bods out of bed to go on watch. The Duty Officers must have been tarred with the same brush as no one ever turned up in the night, the only time we ever saw them was when we were lined up for inspection when the guard was mounted. We were not devoid of sporting personalities as the Commanding Officer was F. E. Greenwood, the former Yorkshire captain, the Flight Officer another cricketer, Austin Matthews of Glamorgan and England whilst our sergeant was 'Sailor' Brown, one of Charlton's greatest footballers.

September 1942 with No. 4 Initial Training Wing at the Grand Hotel, Scarborough — author on right, back row

From Scarborough, I moved to two of the loveliest inland spots in the British Isles, Ludlow and Bridgnorth both set in the Shropshire country-side. The former famous for its castle where John Milton's *Comus* was first performed, I had to read *Comus* for a matriculation paper. Bridgnorth, another fascinating town consisting of two distinct areas, a High and a Low town, and famous for its tower which was part of the original castle which leans from the vertical more than three times as much as the Leaning Tower of Pisa. Service memories are of being under canvas, sharing my bed with earwigs and later when we went into camp, hunking sackloads of coal and peeling hundreds of spuds. I think I should still have been there but for a visiting Air Commodore who enquired how long I had been waiting for aircrew training, thanks to him I was posted the following week. On a sombre note, we attended the funerals of two Canadian airmen killed on a training exercise. They could have hit the Clee Hills which were a notorious flying hazard.

After the summer joys of Shropshire, we travelled north to Whitley Bay where we were attached to the Army for a toughening up commando style course. This didn't go down very well with either myself or my oppos. I was never brought up to roam the fields and byways, eating meals out of billy cans. Throw in a few thunderflashes and crossing rivers on a rope upside down and I reached the nadir of my aspirations. The Luftwaffe also paid us a visit and I found myself lying on top of a plate glass window when a shop front was blown in by blast. All in all I was not sorry to go on Christmas leave in 1943 with all my faculties and physical being intact.

The next stop was the Aircrew Reception Centre better known as 'Arsy Tarsy' in the exclusive suburb of St. John's Wood. This was purely a holding unit but gave us the opportunity to savour something of the night life of the Metropolis. David Tomlinson, the celebrated actor, was a member of our flight and I believe later qualified as a pilot.

We were then shunted to Heaton Park in Manchester where we led another fairly useless existence with the exception of morse lessons and sometimes helping out in a local factory warehouse. This again went on for a matter of weeks and terminated with a church service for our safe crossing of the Atlantic.

3

AIRCREW TRAINING (CANADA)

At the end of May 1943 we left Heaton Park, marched through the main street of Manchester from one station to another and entrained for an unknown destination which turned out to be Liverpool. There under the eagle eye of the Liver bird we embarked, to the rousing strains of a military band on a French liner, the *Louis Pasteur*, named after the famous French chemist, for a six day journey across the broad stretch of the Atlantic which some comforting Jonah said was infested by U-boats. Not being able to swim was cause for apprehension but I had a mate who was an excellent swimmer and pledged himself to look after me. I found to my delight that I was an excellent sailor which came in handy as eighty per cent of our mess deck were so sick that the rest of us got more than our fair share of the rations, including the newly baked bread every day.

Life on board was very amenable, our most exacting duty was the daily boat drill. We whiled away the time playing cards and some vociferous sing-songs in what must have been the main ballroom of the ship. There were no restrictions on parading the decks and with some rough weather developing it was most exhilarating to experience the rise and fall of the ship in some awe-inspiring mountainous seas. Reaching calmer water our enjoyment and complacency received a nasty jolt when the liner came to a sudden stop, a state of affairs which lasted some six hours. Apprehension was not lightened when the crew started dumping wooden boxes overboard and we half expected a periscope to break the surface water and see Curt Jurgens in the conning tower with a loud hailer. Eventually to universal relief the engines started throbbing again and we continued to gaze and wonder at endless miles of ocean zigzagging several times an hour, the pilot's (navigators are called pilots on board ship) plot must have resembled one of those medical scanners which gyrate in opposing polarities so evident in life and death dramas on hospital TV dramas. But one morning we woke to find the fabulous Long Island on our port side. What an impressive and welcome sight; but the peak of emotion was passing the Statue of Liberty, that symbol of freedom, the first harbinger of hope for many thousands of immigrants in the past. We had been scheduled to dock in New Brunswick but an epidemic outbreak caused the authorities to alter their plans.

We saw very little of New York, leaving our berth we were ferried across the Hudson and finally dumped in Grand Central Station. From thence we proceeded to a United States Army Camp near Boston of tea dumping fame for a fantastic few weeks when we were treated like conquering heroes by the people of Massachusetts who were more English than the English. You have only to study the names of some of the towns; Worcester, Cambridge, Manchester, these people were the descendants of the first English settlers. Their homes were magnificent and their generosity was an acute source of embarrassment. Being such a vast country, the sense of distance was non-existent, we could be drinking in one bar and our host would say, let's have another in so and so, which meant a trip of over a hundred miles but the length of the car accounted for the first half mile. I was surprised to find that there were cricket teams over there and stranger than Ripley's fiction, there was a soccer pitch in that world famous academy, West Point. On our travels we passed through Fall River where Mary Borden wielded an axe and Brockton, the home town of the redoubtable Rocky Marciano.

There were no restrictions on the camp and we had no duties to speak of and very few NCOs to push us around. The food was excellent and most hygienically served and one soon got hooked on Coca Cola. The only drawback on the camp were the communal 'loos' with no privacy whatsoever, the reason being that it discouraged suicides, as if anyone would want to. The temperature in the day reached a hundred and twenty degrees and sunstroke was very prevalent, partly due to playing football in the heat of the day in the best traditions of mad dogs and Englishmen. There was quite a goodly number of females of the species to while away the time at station dances but they were well chaperoned and one had to visit a port like Providence to chat up a 'night fighter', which was a waste of good drinking time.

But it all had to come to an end some time and we left with deep regrets this oasis of Anglophiles and travelled north-east to New Brunswick, finding our landfall at Moncton, a town situated on the Petitcodiac river which should have been our original destination. The change of venue was pure bathos, not that the locals were not hospitable but Moncton was no Las Vegas and the inhabitants were inured to the sight of aircrew cadets, so many had passed through on the Empire Training Scheme. Fortunately our stay was not protracted, I scrounged a cushy clerical job and managed to stack away enough dollars to forward some glamour to my wife, presuming Karl Doenitz's marauders didn't interfere. It was at Moncton I learnt a good or bad habit as the idea appeals. We had so much time on our hands that I used to kip down after dinner every day and now it has quite grown on me. To break the monotony, I had the good fortune to meet a former schoolmate who had dropped his anchor in Moncton. He and his wife gave me a right royal evening but it was to be the last I saw of them as two days later my posting to Rivers came through, not that I had ever heard of the place.

And so we boarded a train which was to be our home for the next three and a half days in which we were waited on with meticulous attention by coloured porters. We were embarked on a novel experience which could have been more satisfying if the powers that be had put us in the picture as to what was happening and given us some gen on the itinerary. As it was, we travelled along the shorelines of those vast inland lakes, Huron and Superior, through hundreds of miles of coniferous forests of Ontario until breaking cover in the wheatlands of Manitoba we steamed into the capital, Winnipeg.

Here again, we were overcome by hospitality and alighting on the station to a welcoming crowd we were presented with a card, and I quote: 'These fags and sweets are presented by the Wartime Pilots and Observers Association — a group of Pilots and Observers of the 1914-18 war'. This organization is still flourishing today although there can be few of the originals still left. But our journey was not yet over and we travelled another five hundred miles through a landscape unrelieved by any outstanding features before we pulled into Rivers station, which consisted of one solitary edifice. The town as such is a misnomer, it wasn't even a moderate sized village, consisted of one main street, a few shops and a pub on the corner. White women were at a premium and some of the female population were squaws. The airport itself was situated about two miles away and was skirted by the river Assiniboine which flowed as far as Winnipeg to join Red River and feed into Lake Winnipeg.

We had been posted to the *crème de la crème* as far as navigation training was concerned. It was the No. 1 Central Navigation School and as such was responsible for the efficient running of all the schools in Canada including the training of instructors, the length and material contents of courses, whilst maintaining a close liaison with the navigational requirements of Bomber Command.

Each course was assigned an instructor and in our case it was a middle-aged New Zealander whose job it was to steer us through the course (hopefully). We were taught the basic requirements of navigation, the logic of the triangle of velocities, visual fixtures, the use of the D F loop, astro navigation, taking drift sights, the effect of magnetism in the airframe structure, the variation of the earth's magnetic fields, the art of the Dalton

Airfield at Rivers, Manitoba, with the main runway running through the centre of the picture

No. 1 C. N. S., RIVERS
MEAL CARD
FLYING PERSONNEL

B—0700-0745 D—1230-1330 S—1630-1930

Meal Card for June, 1943 at No. 1 Central Navigation School, Rivers. Meal times displayed on the card

computer (not today's version), how to box a compass and sundry other gems of information, all to ensure a safe passage from A to B in an alien dimension. To me who could only manage a matriculation pass in mathematics it was a real hard slog and I began to wonder if I had picked the right category of aircrew. To add to the trauma, I was not too happy about the flying aspect. I had never been in an aeroplane before in my life, even my wife had beaten me to it, she had been for a five bob flip in Alan Cobham's circus who flew from an airfield at Norton on the outskirts of Sheffield. I wondered what my reaction would be, perhaps I'd be scared, air sick, unable to cope. It is a vastly different proposition navigating an aircraft in the comfort of a classroom with all the time in the world to plot your course than to combat the turbulence, cramped quarters and vagaries of the weather in an Anson which threatened to shed its wings, at any moment.

I needn't have worried. I found it was my metier, in fact it was somewhat cheesing when I did my first trip as a navigator (one flew alternatively as first or second navigator) when the pilot saw a huge black cumulo nimbus cloud directly ahead and decided to call it a day. We could have flown around it but my flight plan did not cater for such an eventuality and the pilot was certainly not disposed to put his one and only life in the hands of a sprog navigator. Anyway, I had actually navigated for an hour and still knew where I was.

Life on the station was pretty humdrum, if we weren't flying we were attending lectures during the day, working on charts at night or taking star shots with a bubble sextant of which the results on the ground were very gratifying but disastrous when airborne. Our free time was spent in the bowling alley or the cinema. Although there was a wet canteen, we conserved our dollars like a monkey storing nuts for the forty-eight-hour passes in Winnipeg where we could billet with some kind locals or book into an hotel. Incidentally, the breakfasts in the hotels after the semi-starvation diets at home were out of this world. I stayed a couple of times with a Danish family who were absolutely super people, the mother was a fantastic cook but the only fly in the ointment was that they liked you to go to church on Sunday morning, and it would have been gross bad manners not to accept their invitation. But it didn't help to have a stinking hangover which was easily acquired in Canada because of the gassy beer.

I had one particular adventure in Winnipeg which is worth relating. In a large departmental store in the centre of the city a band of dedicated women, something akin to the Women's Institute in this country ran a twinning system on a card index principle, the beauty of which enabled them to put you in touch with females who had similar interests to your own. Naturally, one had to reciprocate with one's own idiosyncrasies but beer and crumpet were *de trop* in this context. Given the right answer you were matched up with your female counterpart and given her telephone number. Having satisfied the formalities, I promptly rang my date and arranged to meet her outside the Cave Club, Winnipeg's most popular rendezvous. I asked her how I should recognize her and she said she was very dark and would be wearing a white carnation in her hair. Obviously, this was to be my lucky night but reality was stranger than fiction. I arrived first which was a cardinal mistake and five minutes later she stepped out of a taxi whose plimsoll line took a definite upward trend. She was huge, round about twelve stone, and the carnation by comparison looked like a daisy, dwarfed by what in actual fact was a glorious head of dark wavy hair. Mind you, she might not have been over-impressed with what she saw. The Cave Club was dry, in fact nowhere in Winnipeg could you take a female but I always carried a flask of whisky to lace the Coca Cola and we had a reasonably pleasant and intoxicating evening but strange to say I never used the services of the departmental store again.

Back at the Station, the weather was very hot and it was not the best condition for flying, especially for a navigator who had to wind up the undercarriage by hand which involved about one hundred and twenty revolutions. Few pilots wore a shirt but the privilege was not extended to us despite three hours of flying grind.

One night however nearly saw the end of my flying career. We took off at ten o'clock to drop some practice bombs on the range which was about twenty minutes' flying time away. We dropped the bombs and headed for home but something went drastically wrong. Our time limit was well up and we had seen no sign of the airport so I asked the Skipper if everything was OK. He replied in the affirmative and said that he had picked up the Station beam. But he must have caught up with the back beam and then flew out of it and started doing some wide circles.

After flying for about an hour, we were well and truly lost but after stooging for another hour and a half, we found an airfield, circled it and requested permission to land; but not a peep came out of the place. The pilot should have landed in any case for, although there were no lights, the runway was clearly visible. The field must have been Regina. So off we continued on our odyssey and then the weather clamped with a damp mist forming and we were now fairly desperate as the gas was running low. With gauges mildly oscillating on an ominous zero level, we pierced the overcast, a dicey procedure almost anywhere but Canada. With only the wing tip lights reflecting back the ground fog, faithful Annie touched down but not

Peter Mattingley, the author and Bob Darling in the Cave Club, Winnipeg,
July 1943

before the pilot let out a most disturbing yell at the moment of impact. Within about a quarter of an hour we were surrounded by a crowd, many of whom were Indians. I should have pointed out that we were adjacent to the old Cowboy and Indian country of North Dakota and Montana and some of the places we normally flew over were Medicine Hat, Indian Head, Drunken Point, Dominion City, Snowflake, Fort Qu'appelle, Elk Island, Shoal Lake, all colourful stuff.

We stuck with the aircraft until daybreak when the weather began to clear and accompanied by our strange entourage, we trekked to the local village store and commandeered some cans of fuel. To a cheering crowd, we took off again and returned to base and the inevitable enquiry. I was worried that the incident might have affected my course chances but this proved not to be the case. We had flown five minutes short of five hours, the longest trip I had ever made in an Anson.

Meanwhile, the ground course became more demanding and the subjects we had to cope with included air navigation theory, meteorology, signals, aircraft recognition, photography and log keeping to mention a few.

Then the inevitable happened, we lost two of the course in a flying accident, leaving empty beds in our billet as a constant reminder that flying was not all beer and skittles. Our instructor was very philosophical about the tragedy pointing out that this was one aspect of flying which would always be at our shoulder. All the course attended the funeral and the immortal words of Isaac Watts, penned some two hundred years ago were a fitting epitaph for two good friends and colleagues who would not be returning home:

'A thousand ages in thy sight
Are like an evening gone;
Short as the watch that ends the night
Before the rising sun.

Time, like an ever rolling stream,
Bears all its sons away;
They fly forgotten, as a dream
Dies at the opening day.'

At last, the long slog came to an end and we took our finals, both in the air and on the ground. I managed a pass mark of 83% on ground subjects but only 72% in the air. Well it was all over now and the final fling was a course banquet which was a highly intoxicating affair but nevertheless, it

Daylight trip in an Anson from Rivers, Canada, complete with parachute

was good to let our hair down for a change.

Next morning was Wings Parade when we received our brevets from the commanding officer and a sorry sight some of us were as he pinned on an observer's brevet as no navigators badges were available. In the afternoon, our instructor sent for me and three more who had been my oppos throughout the course and informed us that we had been awarded immediate commissions. But this again was to have tragic results, Bob who had topped the course was automatically chosen to navigate a Lancaster back to England but after taking off from New Foundland was never heard of again.

We returned home in the *Aquitania*, a magnificent four funnelled liner which by a quirk of fate my grandfather had sailed in on several occasions on business trips to America. We docked at Greenock in south-west Scotland and continued by train to Harrogate, that famous spa and elegant town in the West Riding of Yorkshire. Here we underwent further documentation including night vision tests and after what seemed an interminable three days we were shunted off on indefinite leave.

I append some extracts from airgraphs which I sent to my wife from Canada reflecting in some way, the rigours of the course. But it was a deeply satisfying feeling to be a fully fledged navigator and I can think of no better definition of the new status than these observations from an undoubted sage:

'And those navigators — a navigator can find anything. He just takes out some maps, shoots the sun, draws a circle on his map, trisects the circle, figures the number of degrees in each angle against his compass reading, cuts the cards, and before you know it he's located the only blonde in town.'

Bob Hope

AIRGRAPH EXTRACTS

July 8th   I'll be thrilled when I get a four engine job and do a spot of real bombing instead of dropping dummies.

July 9th   I'm so busy flying and working that the time just tears along. Saturdays and Sundays are just the same and we have no spare time.

July 12th   I am working about thirteen hours a day, flying makes you very tired especially if you fly at a good height. I enjoy the flying very much. I'd love to get in a Flying Fortress or a Sunderland.

July 16th   I am mad about flying, the first thing I do in civvy street is to take out a pilot's licence.

We've hardly a minute to ourselves. I started at eight this morning and have just finished, nine-thirty p.m.

July 22nd   I'm doing quite OK but can't find the time to learn all the stuff. Charlie says the course is getting him down somewhat, it certainly is real hard work.

July 24th   I am flying all this week including night flying. We work seven days and nights a week and there is not a minute's let up. My chances of getting a commission are becoming pretty remote. Seventy-five per cent of the class have done advanced navigation and it makes it hard to compete with them and marks count a lot.

July —   I shall be working until about eleven tonight taking star shots. We are having some exams this week. I don't think I have ever known less but you have to cram so much in such a short time.

August 5th   Flying is really great, cherub. I can't imagine anyone being luckier than a fighter pilot. The RAF are doing a great job now, it will be

*Main runway at Rivers, Manitoba, taken
from 5,000 feet*

*Commanding Officer taking salute at Wings Parade, 27 October, 1943,
at Rivers, Manitoba*

quite some time before I get on ops, so don't worry, in any case I just believe in fate. I think I shall get through the course but I can't be too sure.

August —   Sorry this is a day late but have been so busy. I was up till one in the morning taking shots on the stars and had to get up at six to go flying. We got off course today and flew into America but managed to get back home OK. It was a lovely day, we had one continuous mass of white cloud beneath us and couldn't see the ground so I had to take bearings on the sun. I love flying and get a great kick out of it. We have had some exams and I did quite well. I intend to get through this course.

August 7th   In an hour or two I shall be first navigator on a night trip, tearing round a few hundred miles trying not to get lost. I have to wait another month for my next forty-eight and these are the crucial weeks as to whether I get through the course or not. If I fail I shall go as a pilot but I don't intend to fail.

August 13th   Feeling very tired after an exacting week. Last night we got in the plane, the pilot revved the engines and we were just going when the flight was scrubbed owing to bad weather. I am still not sure of getting through the course, I can get round OK in the air but these ground subjects floor me.

August 18th   I was flying last night, the first night back from a forty-eight when I felt like a rest. It was a marvellous night but terribly cold and I was pleased to get to bed. This afternoon we were up again and we are up again tomorrow night so you can see we are just about living in aeroplanes.

August 27th   Sorry to say I'm no heavier, in fact I have lost weight on the course. I just weigh ten stone, we have to work so hard. It's nine o'clock now and the first breather I have taken today. I am going to have a bite to eat and then I shall be taking sextant readings till midnight, my average sleep is six hours. My exams have not gone too well and only the fact that I know I am good in the air makes me stick it. These ground subjects are a nuisance and don't concern the theory of navigation. I'm quite a confident navigator and have every confidence. The commission has gone for a burton as my ground marks are poor, I always have a lot of marks in the air. I'm well down the list on the ground. There is no doubt I shall get it after a few ops. What about the raid on Berlin! Great stuff, what a feeling of achievement those aircrew must have. I'm off to look at the stars now.

August 29th   It is Sunday today and I am working in the classroom with a nice hot sun streaming through the window. I was working very late last night after taking star shots. We had a wizard trip yesterday on a low flying exercise, just the sort of effort you dream about. I did very ropey in the exams although I am putting a lot of work in. I am flying twice tomorrow,

*The author and Eric Herbert in
Montreal Station on the way home
with the help of a Canadian
Pacific loco*

*Eric Herbert, Peter Mattingley,
the author, and Bob Darling outside
our billet at Rivers, Manitoba*

once at night, I really enjoy the flying. I don't know if I shall get to Winnipeg as I am so hard up. I shall go off the station even if it's only thirty miles away because the course is a terrific strain, flying is the easiest part about it.

September 13th   It is raining like mad today. I'm cheesed as we are flying tonight and I don't want it to be washed out. It is Sunday tomorrow but we are having to work although we shall have the morning in bed as we have been flying. I smoke a lot of cigarettes these days but never touch a drink. Still feeling extremely tired darling, I could settle down and sleep for days.

September 15th   Excuse me if I am not writing so often but I am flying and working and I hardly know where I am. I have had quite a lot of pain in my eyes and saw the MO. He said it was due to lack of sleep and due to the course. There are only a few more weeks to go which I can count on my hand but I actually don't know whether I shall pass the course yet. I shall be glad when it is all over as the strain of work is pretty hard.

September 17th   I've got some bad news, it's touch and go whether I make the course or not. I don't know what will happen if I fail, probably be kept on the ground staff. It will be a big blow as I have worked terribly hard. I'm OK in the air but rotten on the ground. We were up five hours the other night, my longest trip so far. I've flown five days or nights out of the last seven and honestly don't know what day of the week it is. It's midnight now and I have hardly looked up since six. We are flying in the morning in an extremely tricky exercise.

I've got seventy-five per cent of my flying time in now and believe there are some hours not logged. I'll be glad when the course is finished or I'm off it, it is a terrific strain and a fight against time all the way.

September 22nd   We took our first final examination this morning and I seemed to do OK but it was comparatively easy. We are flying tonight and tomorrow afternoon. I shall only have seven more trips to do after this. Shall I be glad when this course is over, I have never worked so hard and achieved so little. I lost five pounds in weight in one week, I've got it back again now but I shouldn't like to take anything like this on again.

September 23rd   Just come back from flying, had a very bumpy trip as the weather was poor and it was like being on a switchback. The chap with me was as sick as a dog but it didn't affect me although I have a bit of a headache. I was flying last night so I feel pretty tired but we are off on a forty-eight tomorrow so we shall be able to rest awhile. Still I have only just over a month if I am to make the grade. We have already taken one final and have another one next week.

September 28th   I'm in the middle of swotting but thought it time I dropped you a line. I was flying last night and had quite a good trip. Shall I be glad when this course is over. I lay awake last night thinking of all the things we used to do, cricket matches, students' dances. I don't suppose it will ever be the same again. I shall take up piloting after the war, I think it will be cheap enough, flying will be the thing definitely. I've done more flying now than most of the chaps did in the last war. You don't get very much kick out of this sort of flying but it will be more difficult when we get back to England.

October 5th We had another final exam this morning, one of the last. The great day is dawning nearer. I am flying tomorrow night, should be about next to the last night trip. I just wish I had taken my final C.A. (chartered accountant) I shall be really excited then. I have done so much work for this that it seems an anticlimax. The next ten days we are working full tilt and then we can slack off a bit until the final navigation paper. We are having a flight dinner in just over a fortnight. Everybody gets gloriously tight, financially I shall benefit very little being a sergeant but I dare say your rate of pay will increase.

October — We are having another final tomorrow, another step nearer the day. I have only four more flying trips now and I think it is pretty well certain I shall get my brevet, all being well. I had a pretty ropey trip the other night, we didn't get round too well.

October 14th Only two more flying trips and three more exams. Should be on my way home in a few weeks. Bob however is sure to get his commission (top of the course, killed ferrying an aircraft across the Atlantic) and Pete and I are just as sure not to. These last days are dragging somewhat but it is getting nearer.

*   *   *

This was the last airgraph before I became a fully fledged member of 'The Union' as wartime navigators were known.

But apparently there is still the same jocular camaraderie today as ever. At the time of writing in 1983 a lost Harrier landed on the containers of a cargo ship and inspired the following letter in the *Daily Telegraph*.

AN OLD STORY

Sir,

Vindication at last. We two former Fleet Air Arm Observers have maintained for ages that you can train a chimpanzee to fly but not to navigate.

P. M. Dalton.
P. C. Jewell. London, E.C.2.

4

AIRCREW TRAINING (ENGLAND)

I had a long leave during which I became rather bored, Marjorie was working in a steel works in the east end of Sheffield and there just weren't any people of my age group around. Every morning, I went to the local baths in Heeley and endeavoured to learn to swim but it was to no avail. I had no sense of co-ordination. As a child I spent many months learning to play the piano and my greatest accomplishment was to close the lid. What made it worse at the pool was the arrival of schoolchildren of some tender years, many of whom swam like Olympic champions whilst I floundered like a stranded porpoise. Their arrival was the signal for my departure and a session in the local followed by an afternoon in the flicks. The evenings were more enjoyable as we had the choice of several delectable hostelries and as we were both fond of walking we were never at a loose end. During the course of our travels we palled up with a bomber crew resting from a week on ops and I often wondered whether they survived. The pub was the Robin Hood at Millhouses which was taken over shortly after the war by a good friend, Bill Marsden, a former Sheffield Wednesday wing half who sustained a broken neck in Berlin during a pre-war international.

It came as something of a relief when I got a telegram to report back to Harrogate where I was given a comfortable billet in one of the main hotels. It was good to be back amongst the boys again and we had some gradely nights out in this hospitable and beautiful spa.

At last a posting came through and I had to report to Halfpenny Green situated off the main road between Wolverhampton and Stourbridge. Funnily enough not one of my former colleagues from Canadian days came with me. I have no idea just how many survived the hostilities with the exception of my old mates Peter Mattingley and Eric Herbert who were also commissioned on the course. In 1945, I had a bolt from the blue when Peter invited me to his wedding whilst in the same year I met Eric when I was doing accountancy duties at Melbourne, the home of 'Shiny Ten' Squadron.

My stay at Halfpenny Green lasted only two and a half months and altogether we put in thirty hours flying of which ten were at night. I found night flying in England a very different proposition to Canada where you really couldn't get lost except in circumstances which I have related. Winnipeg was visible for one hundred and fifty miles and shone like a jewelled necklace in the night sky. Over here, it was entirely opposite, nothing but Stygian gloom aggravated by some bloody awful weather, and flying an Anson in those conditions was like riding a bucking bronco.

One of the biggest aids to night navigation were the occulting white beacons situated sparsely around the country flashing a coded morse signal which was changed nightly. The one I used most at Halfpenny Green and operational training unit was Pershore, south-east of Worcester, within easy striking distance of many airfields.

Although flying was somewhat restricted and a great deal of emphasis was put on physical fitness, we still had some good times in the Mess and one of the architects was the sky pilot (padre) who was a real jovial, morale-boosting gentleman of the cloth. It was, however, more diplomatic to drink off the station, as Mess drinks had to be signed for and there weren't any prizes for being top of the league. There was also a curfew which was counter balanced by a gap in the fence which led to one or two skirmishes with the service police.

At this stage in my career, I sported the standard aircrew handlebar moustache and I had arranged to meet a 'night fighter' in the Bell Hotel in Stourbridge. I was waiting patiently quaffing a pint when a load of types from down under bounced into the bar, picked on the first 'pommie bastard' which was me and promptly shaved off the port wing of my hirsute appendage leaving me no alternative but to return to base and complete the job. It was not the only encounter I experienced of Aussies *en masse*, I once shared a hut with a whole crowd of them but I must emphasize that even though they were more than a little on the robust side, their generosity far outweighed all their failings.

The accountant officer at Halfpenny Green was my old colleague who by now had reached the dizzy height of squadron leader and we enjoyed one or two pleasant evenings reminiscing on old times. I wondered then what the circumstances would be when next we met, if ever. The course was too short to be of any practical use as far as flying was concerned but it did afford some idea of the problems of flying in this country. However, I wasn't really sorry when my posting came through to No 21 Operational Training Unit at Moreton-in-Marsh, one of the loveliest spots in the Cotswolds.

This was the catalyst of transforming a sprog flyer into a professional. As yet, we had been playing at being aircrew but this was the moment of truth and here we were moulded into the finished article. At this stage we were all individuals; pilots, navigators, bomb aimers, engineers, wireless operators and air-gunners. Most of the commissioned personnel were either pilots or navigators which could possibly aggravate the problem of crewing up. There was no system, compulsion, or what have you in forming a crew at this stage but since there were far more NCO aircrew than officers, the former had a less difficult task in choosing mates. At least, the composition of aircrew could not have been more democratic.

I fixed myself up with a pilot after dinner on the first night, crews had to be made up in any case the next morning so you had little time to exchange pleasantries. It happened like this. We had a drinking session and I was tanking up with a group of South Africans, there were eight of them all told and one in particular was talking about his first tour in the Middle East. If there is one thing you cannot buy in flying it is experience, so I thought, this is the man for you. Accordingly when he went for a whistle, I followed him and whilst we stood there relieving ourselves, I said, "Have you got a navigator?"

"No," he said.

"Well, you have now," I replied and that was the beginning of an association which took us to many of the main cities in Germany.

Next morning about three hundred of us assembled in a hangar and I and my new Skipper ambled aimlessly about, not really quite certain what to do. But the onus was taken off us when a bomb aimer buttonholed us and offered his services which we accepted with alacrity. He obviously must have got himself organized the night before as he went off and recruited the rest of the crew, bringing each one in turn for our approval. We formed a very cosmopolitan crew, a South African, a New Zealander, a Scotsman, two Yorkshiremen, and one unfortunate who was born on the wrong side of the Pennines. Although we knew nothing about each other at the time, the experiences and traumas of flying as a crew forged a deep bond which I am sure was true of all aircrew, and it is a sad reflection that none of us have communicated with each other since that never-to-be-forgotten day when we finished ops.

Training became much more serious and the flying schedule more onerous. Sometimes I flew as second navigator which was not only a complete waste of time but to my mind it was utterly stupid, since an accident would write off two navigators instead of one. It was also a soul destroying job because as second navigator you were stuck in the middle of the aircraft, starved to death, not able to see anything, performing no useful function at all except pumping oil at odd intervals. This led to an amusing incident some 17,000 feet over the North Sea. The pupil pilot told me to start pumping and the instructor, who was a rank higher, countermanded the order; the pupil of course was a colonial, and then followed a hell of a row with me almost frozen to the pump.

We flew mostly in daylight in the early stages and I had one trip as a second navigator which lasted seven and a half hours. One night a Wellington went missing and then another crashed in a field short of the runway leaving the rear gunner's turret three hundred yards short of the main airframe. We had dinghy drill in the baths at Cheltenham with parachute drill on the station and at the end of the course had to sign a declaration to this effect: 'I am fully conversant with the hydraulic, oil and petrol system including the overload system of the Wellington aircraft.' I didn't even know we had an overload system.

Off duty, we had some great times at Stow-on-the-Wold, Bourton-on-the-Water, Cadbury, Broadway, Chipping Norton, not forgetting the White Hart at Moreton-in-Marsh when an instructor broke his arm and was cheered out of the bar to a waiting ambulance.

About half-way through the course, we were checked out by the squadron leader flying and luck was very much with me that day. We had flown over the Irish Channel in the murk and I was not sure of our position but suddenly we had a break in the cloud cover and I recognized two large chimneys which I had pinpointed on a previous trip as a Shropshire landmark. From this I knew the course to fly back to base like the back of my hand so I passed this on to the Skipper and received a congratulatory slap on the back from our squadron leader instructor when we landed for a fine feat of navigation.

June 6th 1944 was of course D-Day and we spent about three hours in a Wimpey waiting to take off on a training flight, which was eventually cancelled due to the huge amount of aerial activity. At the end of a night trip we used to have fighter affiliation with a Spitfire which made attacks from all quarters to test the Skipper's reaction to the standard procedures for avoidance. Fortunately, as we seemed to spend half our time upside down, my protractor, dividers and pencils were suspended round my neck with string.

Navigation had become much more arduous, since a Wellington could climb up to eighteen thousand feet and as normally wind velocity increases with height, we were supposed to find a new wind every two to three thousand feet so we had a very busy time before reaching our operational height. Our training at the beginning consisted of mostly day flights, chiefly to get us acclimatized to the aircraft and this was combined with a lot of bombing practice. Then we were let loose at night; some of the trips were of quite a long duration involving flights beyond the north of Scotland and well out into the North Sea. Our instructor had dinned it into us to have confidence in our own ability and put implicit trust in the courses we calculated. I followed this maxim against my better judgement one night, flying on an almost direct northerly course; I should have been proceeding over the Cambrian Mountains in Wales but in actual fact we were doing a fair rate of knots up St. George's Channel which fed into Liverpool Bay, and as luck would have it, a convoy must have been forming up because the ack-ack opened up despite our firing the colours of the day.

But the course came to an end in June 1944 and I must admit I was glad to see the back of the Wellington. It was one of the finest of our earlier aircraft and had a wonderful war record, taking part as early as the second day of the outbreak of war to bomb Wilhelmshaven. I disliked it because of the position of the navigator's office which was situated amidships, and even separated from the wireless operator by a door which if shut induced a feeling of claustrophobia. Compensation came in the guise of a month's leave on which I took my South African pilot, and with my wife as guide we explored the Derbyshire Dales and enjoyed the delights of Hathersage, Grindleford, Eyam and Chatsworth, which were all in easy striking distance of my home.

Our next posting, the penultimate before operations, was at the beginning of August when we had the good fortune to be chosen to finalize our flying programme at 1664 Heavy Conversion Unit at Dishforth in North Yorkshire. This was a peacetime aerodrome and after the outbreak of war was the home of several bomber squadrons. It was from here that Wing Commander Pickard of 'Target for Tonight' flew to bomb Wurzburg radar installation at Bruneval. We were not however on the main camp, but housed in Nissen huts at the end of the lane leading to the camp. We converted on to Halifax IIIs which crew-wise was a much superior aircraft to the Wellington. I found it particularly reassuring, as my place was most forward of all the crew and the navigator's seat was spring-loaded. Directly beneath it was the escape hatch, and it would have been possible to vacate the aircraft within ten seconds. In fact I nearly did one night when two engines failed on the same side and we dropped like a stone, then I realized we were over the Bristol Channel and it was a long swim back. We had the usual spate of incidents, one night two Halifaxes reported being attacked over the North Sea but it was eventually proved that they had fired at each other.

It was at Dishforth that I first met one of the 'Guinea Pig' boys when he dined in our Mess. I was caught off balance when I first saw him and gave an involuntary grimace, feeling terribly embarrassed, but he instantly put me at ease saying that everybody had the same reaction. The agonies these men went through in countless operations defies description and was only matched by the stature of Sir Archibald McIndoe and his East Grinstead staff whose dedication and skill enabled so many aircrew to live a normal life again.

The course was much shorter than I expected but I believe the main object was to ensure a smooth transition from twin- to four-engine jobs and the ultimate responsibility devolved on the pilot and the flight engineer. We did a few local flights for acclimatization purposes and I must say that I found the aircraft much to my liking, with plenty of room to move about for a change.

For the first time I became aware of the peculiar smell indigenous to the interior of all Halifaxes, consisting of a mixture of petrol, oil, aircraft dope, oxygen, and kindred other aircraft components — something I have never experienced since. We progressed to fighter affiliation and the way the instructor threw the aircraft about the sky, one could have been forgiven if they thought he had a death wish. The acid test came with three long night trips, all over six hours duration, culminating in a mock bomber attack which turned out quite successful. We were graded again and I was assessed as average which I think applied to the crew as a whole, although it was my log-book which was endorsed by the chief flying instructor. On reflection, I should imagine this was the standard observation as it would hardly boost one's confidence if they wrote 'below average'.

A most interesting feature which didn't come to light until many months later was that the instructors guessed at the life expectancy on operations of crews that passed through their hands. We must have made a big impression, as they prophesied the 'chop' for us within six trips.

5

OPERATIONAL

The training was now all behind us and we waited for news of our posting, not without some trepidation, I might add. We did not have far to go, a train journey to the beautiful walled city of York, steeped in almost two thousand years of history, which was to be my happy stamping ground for the next two years. Here we were picked up by RAF transport which took us down the main Beverley-Hull highway until we came to the Officers' Mess, which fringed the junction of the main road and the side turning into the village of Pocklington, nestling at the foot of the Yorkshire Wolds. This was the home of 102 Squadron, 4 Group, Bomber Command where Cheshire earned his first DSO, bringing back a kite with half its fuselage shot away. We were not aware of this at the time, and our enthusiasm had been somewhat dented by the sight of two pranged Halifaxes indecorously sprawled in fields adjoining the main road. There was practically no one around as we alighted and were directed to our billets. In actual fact there was a stand down which meant no operations on that day or night and which we learnt later was a *carte blanche* pass to indulge in the sybaritic delights of Eboracum (York). Being a wartime airfield opened in June 1941, the accommodation was not lavish, and I was installed in the now familiar barrack hut. This time it was partitioned off, so that two officers could share a room. It did cross my mind that my predecessor may have got the chop or gone missing or more hopefully finished his tour, I did not think it politic to enquire too closely.

Having unpacked, I picked up the Skipper and we retired to the Mess which was less than a hundred yards away for the afternoon 'char and wad' session. We had hardly sat down before receiving a hearty welcome from a three-ringed job who turned out to be the CO himself, Wing Commander L. D. Wilson — 'Willy' for ever after — who at this time sported a DFC and an AFC. His welcome was more than unusually warm, chiefly I think because Gerry was a South African, and an Army officer with wings on a bomber squadron was not exactly a daily occurrence. At the time, I did not feel very much at ease and I felt less so when another officer came in and whispered to the CO, whereupon he turned round and shouted, "I want him off the station by tonight." Apparently this particular officer had gone

LMF (lack of moral fibre). In layman's terms he just hadn't the guts to fly any more. These aircrew deserved a lot of sympathy but at that time sympathy did not win wars, and since it was an infectious syndrome, such personnel had to be summarily discarded. But it certainly did not make me feel much happier, I might be another LMF case myself.

Next day I reported to the navigation section and met Phil Morris, the Nav Leader who was to be my mentor and friend for the next six months and to whom I owe an everlasting debt of gratitude for his advice and encouragement which saw me through my tour. In his office was a large chart with all the navigators' names written on it followed by crayoned blocks for each completed trip. A thicker line signified an ominous end to some of the names.

But the serious side came with a night cross country which might sound perfunctory but involved several hours flying, the object was to see whether my navigation was up to scratch. I managed to get round and land at the right airfield whilst Gerry was careful enough not to make a hole in the runway. The following evening, we were told to report at 19.30 for a job tied up with the main force. It was our baptism of fire, an initiation to operational flying. Briefing was very informal as it was a one crew, one trip only job. To summarize, we were to be decoys for the main stream. The object of the exercise was to create a diversion and draw the German fighters on to us. We were to fly to Caen and I must say the idea did not appeal very much to me. Conditions however were perfect, there was not a breath of wind and, as a feat of navigation, it was a non starter. Apart from Gee, it was a perfect area for H2S with Le Havre and the River Seine on the port beam and if you strayed too far to starboard, there was the unmistakeable Cherbourg Peninsula.

We didn't hang around Caen too long and I gave the Skipper a reciprocal course to return to base. My Mercator chart showed two coincident straight lines from Pocklington to Caen and back. At least I gained some fame from my non navigational exploit as the chart was suitably framed on the wall of the Nav Leader's office and was still there when I left Pocklington several months later.

We had now been accepted as an operational crew and six days later we were detailed for our very first operation, Brest, where the *Scharnorst* and *Gneisenau* had their base until 1942 when they succeeded in dashing up the English Channel in daylight. But now it was the port itself which was still a main threat to shipping. Incidentally, the harbour was built by Richelieu as far back as 1631. Imagine then our feelings, never been in action before, briefed for a tough daylight target. On the way out, some of the tension

102 Squadron, Navigation section

*The crew — L. to R. (back row) Harry, Jock, author, Colin
(front row) Steve, Gerry and Larry*

rubbed off as one looked around and saw nothing but line upon line of Halifaxes as far as the eye could see. And then, over the target area we experienced our very first taste of flak. I can only describe it as fascinating, the shells burst in lazy mushrooms of black smoke which really looked quite innocuous. Later on in the tour, experience soon taught us to recognize the danger signals in daylight. At night you had no yardstick. If the core of the mushroom was red, it was too close for comfort and again it was only experience which could influence you in deciding whether to climb or drop a thousand feet. That in my opinion, was the reason many survived a tour or more whilst others went for a burton after only a few trips.

Nobody could guard against a burst of flak or cannon shell killing the pilot but an experienced crew could minimize or overcome the effects of enemy action. It is no secret that the standard evasion from an attack by a fighter was to corkscrew starboard and port dropping and recovering height to remain on course but fortunately we were never singled out for a fighter attack. During the whole of my operational career I saw very few fighters. I was in the nose of the aircraft one night when a Junkers 88, easily recognizable by its radial engines appeared head on and shot above us, even the Skipper never saw it. The only other times we had cause for alarm was when M E 262s, jet propelled jobs, buzzed the bomber stream in daylight. These were fantastic aircraft fitted with R4M rockets of super lethal power. They were the first operational jet fighters capable of over five hundred miles an hour and there is no doubt that if the Luftwaffe had oncentrated on this aircraft earlier, Bomber Command would have suffered much heavier losses. These kites were capable of taking off from autobahns and their most famous pilot was General Adolf Galland, probably the most celebrated flier Germany ever produced, with the exception of the 'Red Knight', Baron Manfred von Richtofen.

But this trip proved a piece of cake as far as fighters and flak were concerned, and in less than five minutes we were through target area and out over the safety of the Atlantic. A wide turn of over one hundred and eighty degrees brought us safely on the home course. Our first encounter with the enemy was over.

So now we were blooded, our next trip was another daylight, we were briefed to wipe out a doodle bug site at La Pourchinte, an operation dear to the heart. The doodle bug and the more sophisticated V2 were used without any discrimination whatsoever chiefly because of the lack of technical know how, and it was anyone's guess where they finally landed. It was not a deep penetration into France and though there was patchy cloud over the dropping area we had no problem in picking out the red target indicators.

Bombing raid on La Pourchinte doodle bug site — Narrative: 1st September 1944, height 14,000 feet. Bomb load — nine 1,000lb bombs and four 500lb bombs. 'G' for George, 102 Squadron. To the left of centre are buildings, all roofless. At the bottom right-hand corner, target indicators can be seen burning

Some radar predicted flak was encountered but of no consequence although one aircraft had its nose canopy shattered but fortunately, no casualties. The whole trip took only three and a half hours and I spent the afternoon at the flicks in York, had a snack in Betty's Bar and finished up tripping the light fantastic at Fred Keech's in a haze of alcoholic euphoria.

Two days later, the fifth anniversary of the outbreak of war, saw us in another daylight and this time the target was Venlo, the specific aiming point being the airfield. Venlo stood on the river Maas and was one of the frontier towns of the East Netherlands. It was strategically important because of its proximity to the industrial Ruhr but it was a reprehensible target from my point of view because the town was renowned for its brewery. I should have refused to go on ethical grounds. It was a typical late summer day and we had an uneventful trip out but encountered some very heavy flak in the target area and were holed in several places. With the weather deteriorating and losing an engine we were diverted to North Creake where we were able to inform the intelligence officer that we had bombed visually and actually seen our load burst on the runway. After kipping down for the night in one of those half circular Nissen huts we returned by train to York and in the process came in for some quite unwarranted fuss from fellow passengers which was good for the ego.

We had a respite of over a week before being stuck on another Ruhr target in daylight, Nordstern situated right in the heart of the Ruhr. It was a high priority target because of its oil production, but it was also heavily involved in coal, iron, steel and engineering. This trip was most memorable for the intense flak, without doubt the heaviest we had encountered, and we lost an engine for the second time in succession. The problem with these targets in the centre of the Ruhr was the unlimited concentration of flak in whichever direction you turned, and the most dangerous moments followed the release of the bombs then allowing two minutes for the photo flash before making an abrupt change of course to guide the aircraft on the home run. And all the time, the flak is hitting the aircraft with a ratatat like a shower of hail. On one trip a fierce burst showered on the airframe and I felt a distinct thud in the back of my heel. After the sensation wore off, I could feel the warmth of blood, and dutifully informed the Skipper I had been hit but there was no problem in carrying on. Arriving back at base I gingerly removed my shoe and was shocked to find no damage. On closer examination, there was a slit in the leather and embedded inside was a lump of flak, so on future trips I took my own flak with me. At least, I had learnt the meaning of the word psychosomatic.

The following week we lost an aircraft in very unusual circumstances when it failed to return from a practice bombing exercise over the North Sea. As far as I know there was no logical explanation unless the details were kept secret and it seems extraordinary that there was no mayday call, wreckage, or bodies recovered. The pilot was a South African and as there were only eight on the squadron his loss on a non-operational exercise together with his crew in such unfortunate circumstances was deeply felt.

It was a bit of a ritual when someone went missing; as I said before, two officers shared a room with a batman to do all the cleaning and in my case ensure there were some bottles of Guinness to hand when I returned. Once it was established that your room mate would not be returning, some bod came along and removed all his gear making sure that the other occupant was either on an op or in York. In one instance, they not only removed my room mate's kit but my shaving gear as well which ended up in the local mortuary. In case I did not return, I always made a point of putting all my money in an envelope addressed to my batman. Some nights he could have been well off. The casualty rate was insidious and didn't really register unless you went on leave and learnt that so and so had gone missing whilst you were away. In any Mess, whether it was training or operational, it was not the done thing to talk about accidents, fatal or otherwise. I was fortunate to be flying at a time when casualties were at their lowest, but one has only to realize that if one aircraft went missing out of twenty on an op, then the remaining nineteen would be out on the next night and over a period of thirty to forty missions, it could be very much a 'ten little nigger boys' syndrome.

Having been on the station over a month we were given a week's leave which I spent with the wife in Morecambe making the usual trip to the Lake District, a holiday which ensured another generation of the Rodgers family. I certainly hadn't missed out on anything back at Pocklington as the squadron had been engaged on ferrying petrol to Melsbroek, each plane carrying seven hundred and fifty gallons a time, and it certainly wouldn't have found favour with one of the gunners who was wont to indulge in a crafty drag in his turret.

Back on the treadmill, we found ourselves airborne on another daylight to bomb plant and oil installations at Scholven and took a real pasting from the defences, being holed in several places, as were other aircraft in the squadron. There was no cloud in the target area and several large explosions were seen on the plant. For the first time we encountered enemy jet propelled aircraft but in the laconic words of the official record — 'Supporting Spitfires soon set about them and drove them away'.

It was good to tuck another op under our belt as my room mate went missing on Munster and we had lost some good friends in quick succession. He had only been recently commissioned and requested to share a room with me as we had been friends at conversion unit. He had only survived a few trips giving credence to the theory that the first half-dozen operations presented one of the most dangerous periods of a tour.

The next target was purely strategic and had English connotations as it was the birthplace of Anne of Cleves, the fourth wife of that sexual gourmet, Henry VIII. In north-west Germany it was known as Kleve and was renowned mostly for its production of footwear, but in October 1944 it was a stumbling block to the Allied advance being replete with troops and armour. Since our infantry and armoured corps were within striking distance of the town, the bombing had to be precise. Although there was a layer of stratus above us we were able to bomb visually and on the markers. The concentration was very marked and smoke from the fires could be seen one hundred and fifty miles away when we crossed the coast in the Antwerp region. Two aircraft were seen to go down in the target but not from our squadron. It was a sad moment on an operation when one of the crew reported an aircraft going down as it was the navigator's job to log the number of crew bailing out, latitude, longitude and aircraft identification if possible. Things happened so fast however and travelling at four miles a minute it was not possible to make dispassionate observations. The uppermost thought — there but for the grace of God, go we.

A week later it was the city of Duisburg the world's largest industrial inland port situated on the Rhine with roughly a population of half a million, a very strategic target being heavily involved in steel, engineering and shipbuilding. Approximately a thousand of us went and encountered only token opposition. We bombed from just under twenty thousand feet and noted a pillar of reddish brown smoke but apart from the heavy ack-ack over the target, the only other problem was to avoid crossing either Krefeld or Dusseldorf on the way out. When we returned to base we were astounded to learn that another op was on that night and the target, believe it or not was again Duisburg. As we had done three ops in eight days, we were not on the crew list but several others were detailed for the second op in less than twenty-four hours. The operation was a piece of cake, the defences had been saturated and the target was still on fire from the daylight raid, the flames could be seen from one hundred and fifty miles away and navigators were surplus to requirements. It must have been a terrible experience for the population with over two thousand four-engine bombers almost blasting the city off the face of the earth. People talk about German raids over England but the maximum effort of five hundred twin-engine Heinkels,

The picture we brought back from Scholven. 6th October, 1944. Height 17,200 feet, heading 116 True. Sixteen 500-lb bombs. Lt Meyer, 'F' for Freddie, 102 Squadron

Junkers 88 and Dorniers pales into insignificance relative to the armageddon which convulsed the Third Reich. From our point of view, it was a very successful double operation as not one single squadron aircraft was lost.

Bomber Command and the United States Eighth Army Air Force have been criticized in retrospect for the casualties inflicted on civilians and this particularly highlighted by Nagasaki and Hiroshima. As far as aircrew were concerned it was a completely dispassionate job and I am absolutely certain that nobody thought of the consequence of unloading twelve thousand pounds-worth of bombs. The horror and consequent mutilation was never envisaged, to us it was a cross on a map or a dot in a circle, somewhere to get away from as quickly as possible. Because of the advancement in sophisticated weapons and scientific technology it was inevitable that war meant total involvement, and the ultimate criterion is that the present day critics who were not around at the time would certainly have not been here today if these events had not happened.

We were out again the following night and it was a crucial time for me; we hadn't flown at night for two months and the target was Wilhelmshaven, an important port in north-west Germany specializing in oil refinery, machinery, and chemicals, besides being an important naval base. So it was with some trepidation on my part when we took off. Any bloody fool can get around in daylight but the night reveals nothing but a Stygian darkness which can only be exploited by applying the knowledge of long hours of training. Navigation however, at this period of the war, was reasonably sophisticated, the chief aid was Gee, a device which transmitted pulses from two slave stations situated at strategic points in the United Kingdom which calibrated a mileage, reflecting a green fluorescent image on a screen in front of the navigator. The two images were juggled until they came together and the readings on the screen were translated on to a main chart composed of intersecting lines of purple and red, and where the two lines crossed was your position. The other main aid, H2S was an instrument comparable to a television screen, pulses were beamed down from a cupola situated in the belly of the aircraft and bounced back from the earth like a sorbo ball. Solid objects such as coast lines, land and towns gave a positive response and showed up on the screen as a phosphorescent reproduction of the terrain below, accentuated by the black background of the circular picture. A navigator was up against two problems, first of all Gee was only effective for a short way across the North Sea before the German radar stations jammed the transmissions with grass rendering the set useless. So at a minimum one had to travel two to three hundred miles on dead reckoning especially on a long sea crossing. Short of radar assistance it was a

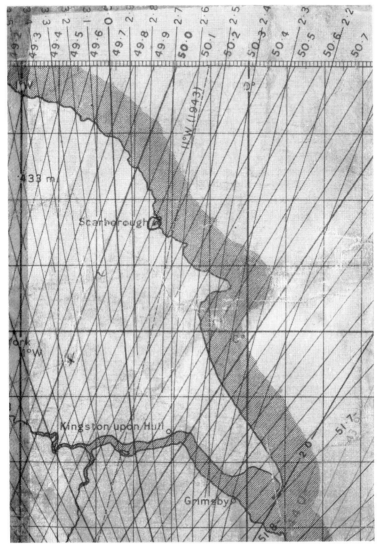

A Gee chart. The map is a section of a Gee chart used by navigators to fix the position of the aircraft. Pulses were read off the screen of the Gee Box and the resultant figures transferred to a main chart. Example: 50.2 and 2.77 is Scarborough. These charts could be used over France and Germany but the transmissions were heavily jammed by German counter radar

worrying time, so I sat with my eyes glued to the H2S screen waiting for the very first response to track in from the right. I was dead in luck, the East Frisian Islands, off the north-west coast of Germany were the first to show. I was spot on track for the target. Flying a course of ninety degrees I swung the camera into line with the radar screen and as Colin dropped our load at nineteen thousand feet I simultaneously clicked the camera shutter, gave the Skipper a rapid and violent change of course to evade the probing searchlights, bags of boost and in a matter of minutes, we were on a Blighty course again.

We climbed to take advantage of the prevailing wind and went like a bat out of hell for home, a glowing feeling of another job behind us. Half-way across the North Sea, time for coffee and chocolate, switch on the IFF (Identification Friend or Foe) not much joy being shot down by your own ack-ack. We gradually lose height and cross the Yorkshire coast at two thousand feet, south of Flamborough Head, spot the welcoming flashing red morse signal from base beacon, join the base circuit, then follows the intercom patter which is pure nostalgia:

"Hello Clearstream, Hello Clearstream, F for Freddy calling — May I pancake please?"

"Hello F for Freddy, Clearstream calling, receiving you loud and clear. QFE one zero one two (barometric pressure at ground level which is fed into the altimeter to ensure the correct height). You are clear to land, runway 32, wind on starboard."

We complete our circuit and turn into the funnel, height now fifteen hundred feet, thirty-five degrees of flap, airspeed one-forty, undercarriage down, through the outer marker beacon, height now seven hundred, airspeed one hundred and thirty-five. Inner marker beacon comes up, we are now at two hundred feet, airspeed a mere one hundred and twenty-five and falling, flaps fully down, the runway stretches ahead flanked by two rows of lights which almost seem to join at the end. A bit of gun, a slight bump and a shudder as sheels touch *terra firma*, a perfect landing, nice one Skipper.

Down to the De-briefing, where the sky pilot (padre) gives you a steaming hot cup of coffee generously laced with rum and then the usual spiel to the intelligence officer, a sensuous soak in a hot bath, a couple of bottles of Guinness and final surrender into the arms of Morpheus.

Hanover should have been our next night target but after covering two hundred miles of our outward journey we were recalled for some unknown reason, which was a very depressing occurrence after having gone through all the traumas of hanging about all day and getting one's self into the correct frame of mind. What is more, it did not count towards a tour and often it was the preliminaries which were more nerve-racking than the actual trip.

At this stage of my tour my wife arrived and booked in at the local pub, very friendly people but due to wartime restrictions, very little heat. Strictly speaking, she was liable to be called up or directed into employment. She had however given up her job on her own accord as a shorthand typist at Hadfields, one of the bastions of steel and armaments in Sheffield, and a very understanding local labour exchange gave their blessing to her staying at Pocklington. It was a contentious move in more ways than one since it put a certain amount of onus on me but a lot more on her, counting aircraft coming back from a raid was not one of the lighter sides of operational life and could also be very misleading. However, we managed to find a billet at Allerthorpe which was half a mile down a lane from the Officers' Mess. We were made very welcome by the landlady and her small child and with her husband being away in the Army, she was grateful for the company, an ideal situation to our mutual advantage. It made a welcome change from the camp and this was the first time we had lived together since our marriage in forty-two.

I was completely breaking regulations living outside the camp without permission but I established a bush telegraph in case of emergency which only happened once. Wives and girl-friends were not welcome in the eyes of the authorities, a sentiment with which no one would disagree. I remember one painful occasion when a crew bought it on the same raid I had been on and I was deputed the unenviable job of breaking the news to one of the wives who had come to spend the weekend at Pocklington and it was not a duty I look back on with relish.

But authority did turn a blind eye. When my wife was staying at the Feathers, I was trekking down the lane, past Pocklington School to the camp when a Humber drew up sporting the pennant of the Base Commander. It was the Air Commodore himself, known affectionately by all aircrew in 4 Group as 'Gus'. I thought I'd blown it this time, I didn't even have the excuse of taking the dog for a walk and in any case they were *persona non grata* on the station. But I could not have been more wrong. He had taken a particular interest in the South African contingent and knew that I was in one of the crews, so I was able to fill him in regarding the ops we had done to date, and I must say his chat was a great morale booster. If only I could have known then that I would be one of his assistants at Heslington Hall in six months' time.

Some more information about the cottage. I should point out that in the winter of forty-four it was so cold that the water froze in the hot-water bottle. And what's more, there was no running water and we had to use a pump. The biggest drawback was having a bath as all the water had to be boiled, it was no problem for me since I had the facilities at the camp but my wife who was a bathomaniac spent most of the night boiling kettles. It was a large tin bath and my main recollection is falling into it after a convivial night in the Mess and being unable to climb out.

Our third successive night trip saw us bound for Essen, one of the biggest cities in the heart of the Ruhr, famous for the Krupp's armament factory. The weather was just unbelievable, we literally fought through twenty thousand feet of cloud, ice, snow and sleet whilst St. Elmo's fire danced along the gun barrels in a blue fluorescent display which would have been eye-catching under other circumstances. The gyro compass and repeaters went for a burton and the Gee was quite useless. I was really lost, the only thing working was the ordinary compass and I couldn't be too sure about that.

I must confess that I was near to panic, flying blind, Christ knows where in Germany, I knew there was something terribly wrong. On a normal trip at night, if you cannot see any other aircraft, you can feel the occasional bump of somebody else's slipstream so you know you are thereabouts in the right place. We should have seen the target indicators going down by now but there was just nothing. Steve the engineer reported that we had used up a lot of fuel but Gerry, the Skipper, said we'll give it another ten minutes. I didn't see any point in this, we were past the target time and nothing was going to show up now. Gerry and I had a bit of an argument and I threatened to bale out if we carried on much longer which brought in the rest of the crew who backed me up. So we did a smart about turn and so did our fortunes, the H2S rebounded with some good responses. We were well north of Essen but I was able to identify München-Gladbach where we jettisoned our load and brought an active response from the anti-aircraft guns but were soon out of range. Fighter activity must have been completely negligible because we must have stuck out like sore thumbs on the German radar screens. Our main worry now was the fuel problem besides having two engines playing up, and there was no chance of making base. We altered course for Manston on the Kent coast which had one of the longest and widest runways in the United Kingdom. Leaving the lowering of the flaps and undercarriage until the last moment before touchdown ensured a safe landing with so much tarmac in reserve. The following morning we trooped out to the aircraft and the fitter said we only had enough fuel left for fifteen minutes flying. If we had flown another ten minutes into Germany, I shouldn't be writing this account now.

We were now stuck at Manston whilst they repaired the engines and took full advantage of the break to whoop it up in Ramsgate. The night before we left, we went to a hop in the town and fell in with another stranded bomber crew. Somewhat worse for wear, we hired a taxi back to camp. Half-way there the cabby stopped and said there were too many in the taxi. He could just have been right as there were some bods on the top. However he made a bad technical error and stepped out of the ill-used vehicle in a gesture of defiance whereupon a gunner stepped into the driving seat and whisked us back to camp. A complaint was made next day but as we were scheduled to leave nothing was made of it apart from one senior officer commenting he was glad to see the back of us.

Next afternoon, 'Fanny by Searchlight' was ready to go and after the Skipper had signed the Form 700 we taxied round the perimeter track until the seemingly never-ending runway stretched out in front of us. The Skipper and the engineer went audibly through the take off check list, T for trimming tabs, M for mixture control, P for propellor speed control, F for fuel, F for flaps, supercharger in M, gills open one third and air intake cold. A standard take off, the throttles were opened slowly and eased to the gate as the aircraft accelerated. At just over a hundred miles an hour we were airborne when catastrophe struck and two engines cut on one side. This was normally the kiss of death but Gerry handled it masterly; cutting all the throttles we bounced back on the runway, bounced up again two or three times. The aircraft was completely out of control now as we ran off the runway, but after a scary two or three minutes, it could have been much less but seemed more like three hours, we eventually came to rest. The next day my room mate brought down another Halifax from Pocklington and ferried us back without further incident. Later Gerry received a commendation from 4 Group for his handling of the situation.

PRELIMINARIES TO A RAID

Life on a Bomber Command station rode the whole gamut of emotion from the euphoric gaiety of Mess party to the sombre and sobering reality of flying the night skies over the Third Reich and hoping it was not your night for the chop.

I can't say I ever lost any sleep wondering whether I would be on operations the next day or night and I can say with complete conviction that my operational tour was one of the least stressful periods of my life. As a child and an adolescent, I was always of a nervous disposition. A report in

Aircrew Soccer XI, — author's crew provided three members. He is first on the left, next to him is Colin the bomb aimer, and next but one is Jock the mid upper gunner

Group Captain D. O. Young, DSO, DFC, AFC, presenting Squadron Cup to Aircrew Captain — Ron Mills, air gunner)

1947 published by the Air Ministry showed that there was an average of around three thousand cases a year of nervous breakdowns amongst flying personnel and around fifteen per cent of accepted aircrew were predisposed to this condition, but fortunately of this percentage, many adapted successfully to war-time operational flying.

The day began with a wakey-wakey call from the batman armed with a steaming cup of tea as some compensation to alleviate the stale smell of a stove which had long since gone out. Shaking off a hangover which was not too hard in those younger days, one ambled to the Mess and indulged in a hearty breakfast reminiscent of the sentiments attaching to the gallows prisoner, whilst our own demise was not quite as certain. Then a quiet stroll to the navigation section, we were far beyond such outmoded, abhorrent, and anti-human activities such as parades.

Down at the section, it was a matter of privilege where you disported your body. Only the veterans and this would be no more than three were allowed in the sanctum of the Navigation Leader's office. There we smoked endless cigarettes, told unprintable jokes, discussed types we liked and the opposite, waiting all the time for the black telephone in the corner to spit out its message which could be a matter of life or death to some aircrew. Sometimes it was a stand down which meant a sortie on York, the main target being Betty's Bar where one could meet all one's cronies operating from other stations in the Group.

But if the powers that be in Bomber Command at High Wycombe got the all clear from the meteorological wizards then it meant another night on the treadmill of fate. A chain reaction was set up by Air Chief Marshal Sir Arthur Harris surrounded by his acolytes, a target was chosen after much discussion and relayed on the scrambler to all Groups which in due course filtered down to the squadrons where the message was "Maximum effort tonight." Bomber Command were in business once more.

We dispersed to the Mess after passing the message to the other members of the crew enjoying a lie in. Then followed the worst part of the operations; we didn't know the target, all outgoing telephone calls were cancelled, incoming calls were monitored whilst armourers, fitters, cooks and half the station were rounded up for the maximum effort.

After lunch, we mooned about the Mess, some played cards, some billiards, most read papers and out of date magazines which they had read before, the words didn't really register. About the middle of the afternoon the bomb load appeared carried on a long low train and the engineers amongst us quickly calculated the load. High loads and low fuel tanks usually meant the Ruhr or West Germany whilst a converse loading could mean Hanover, Berlin or Leipzig.

That was the reason I preferred the Halifax to the Lancaster, we just did not have the capacity for the longer trips. Time was interminable, a curious vacuum of the mind with one part willing the minutes and hours away whilst hoping against hope that the tannoy would announce that the operation had been scrubbed. Relief came as a welcome hiatus around half-past four in the form of a light tea with more small chat and banter, but underneath the surface a nagging sensation of fear.

Navigators' briefing was probably the most important of the individual briefings and around five o'clock the embryo descendants of Columbus and Magellan made their way to the navigation section, which was a very sparsely equipped hut consisting of around thirty utilitarian benches on which we unrolled our Mercator charts, the open sesame to Germany. On the far wall was a huge map of Europe and from a red backed cylindrical pin stuck in the co-ordinates of Pocklington a red cotton meandered its way in straight lines with changing angles until it came to rest on the target, and then by another circuitous route found its sanctuary like a homing pigeon in the metaphorical loft of Pocklington.

The target site either frightened you or anaesthetized the insidious feeling you had been carrying in your stomach since you first knew that ops were on. But now, there was work to be done. The Navigation Leader Phil Morris took over, we were given the routes, turning points, anticipated winds, air speeds, times on each leg, time on target, normally a latitude of two minutes either side of zero hour. The time to collate all this information usually took up about half an hour but in stress terms a minimum of ten Woodbines. And then on to the main briefing to join the rest of the crew, some of whom learnt the location of the target for the first time. The Station Commander, as in all the best movies, would march in with his staff and make the introductory remarks, followed in turn by the specialist officers who would give us the benefit of their views. The Intelligence Officer would inform you that there would be little flak in such and such an area, a remark guaranteed to raise guffaws. The Met Officer would warn of some hazy cloud on return to base which was a polite way of saying you would probably return to a pea-souper. The ceremonies ended with the synchronization of Omega watches, then back to the Mess for bacon and egg. As we left, we passed a table by the main door which held a bowl containing innumerable white pills. They were not drugs to make you think flak was cotton wool but common or garden 'Wakey-wakey pills' guaranteed to keep you awake for hours. I can't imagine what sort of aircrew needed a stimulus to keep awake over enemy territory with the exception of the bods

York Minster which author's crew used to circle before setting course on a daylight raid. 5 Group on Lancasters used Lincoln Cathedral

who shot down the night fighters in the bars and dance halls of York.

Down to the locker room to pick up all the gear, colours of the day, chocolates, sweets, thermos flasks and a change into electric suits for the gunners. I never wore any flying clothes and in fact on many occasions wore my best blue and carried a brief-case with pyjamas, change of attire, not forgetting the shaving kit. Then outside piling into three-ton lorries to be dropped by a WAAF driver at the various dispersal points. There the ground crew would be waiting and what great people they were, they virtually carried our lives in their hands and to them our aircraft, 'F' for Freddy was a well beloved symbol on which they lavished their care and devotion and there was always that last plea, "For Christ's sake — don't bend it."

Few people have ever appreciated the complicated routine involved in getting a bomber airborne. The bomb load varied between eight and twelve thousand pounds and the maximum fuel capacity was just over eighteen hundred gallons which the engineering section permuted in relation to the calculated mileage. At dispersal, the first checks were pretty academic, but being so obvious could so easily be overlooked and, as usual, familiarity bred contempt. The first and foremost ritual was the pitot head, a rod situated at the end of the wing which fed into the airspeed indicator, failure to remove the cover was the quickest way to meet St. Peter. Follow this up with a walk round the aircraft to check for oil and fuel leaks, make sure the cowlings were secure, inspect the tyres for cuts or creep and then it's all aboard, not forgetting the last earthbound 'whistle'. Once inside the aircraft each member checked his own station. In my case, it was the Gee box, the H2S, the gyro compass, check your bag for protractor, calculator, maps and charts, a good supply of pencils and make sure the tiny light over the chart table worked. There never was a great future in plotting in total darkness. But it was on the flight deck that most of the checks had to be made and there was a standard check list procedure to be followed which is too complicated to explain fully. Having completed all the checks it was now necessary to start the engines and to expedite this a ground battery was plugged into the engine. Each engine was turned by hand at least two revolutions, the ignition was switched on, the starter and booster coils pressed and the engine like a pistol shot burst into life. Each engine was revved up to one thousand revolutions per minute, the ground battery was disconnected and we were now in business. In our case we had to cross the road from dispersal and often had a crowd of well-wishers to see us off. It was possible to stand on the brakes, give a boost on either the port or starboard engine and some unfortunate night fighter would find her skirt above her head.

We joined the long queue of aircraft snaking around the perimeter track until it was our turn at the end of the runway. Standing on the brakes, the engines were run up to maximum capacity and throttled back again, we got a green from the aldis lamp of the controller, the throttles were opened slowly at first then fully, the aircraft accelerated, the tail coming up easily as speed developed and at one hundred and thirty miles an hour and two-thirds down the runway, we were airborne and the first hurdle had been cleared. Germany, here we come.

On the thirtieth of October we made our first trip to Cologne, one of the largest cities on the Rhine, famous in peacetime for its Eau de Cologne and its Gothic cathedral, but industrially it was a seething hive of industry with its machinery, chemicals, metallurgy and oil refining, besides its strategic importance as a centre of communications. We took off at five to six in the evening and touched down a minute before midnight which was a fair old jaunt for a target within reasonable striking distance, but the route planning was designed to leave the identity of the night's target as late as possible. With this end in mind, spoof raids were sent almost every night to fox the defences and it was very much a battle of the 'boffins' as to the success of the night's operations. This was a particularly easy trip and although there was ten-tenths cloud over the target, there was no difficulty in picking out the sky markers.

Three nights later, we went to Dusseldorf which was more or less the kingpin of the industrial Ruhr, it manufactured anything from iron and steel to cars and textiles. There was a moon that night and we told the gunners to be particularly watchful. As it turned out there was a fair amount of searchlight, flak and fighter activity but thankfully we were never involved. German fighters used to orbit beacons and were then vectored on to the bomber stream by ground control, but this was not always successful as there were visibility problems. Their boffins then came up with Liechenstein which consisted of radar antennae fixed on the nose of the fighter enabling the pilot to home on the bomber. They also developed a device known as Naxos which homed on to the H2S signals coming from the bomber. We were advised to use this navigation aid as little as possible over enemy territory but I am afraid at times, due to expediency, I ignored this warning and switched on to confirm our position. This night however was very clear and we bombed the target indicators and saw many fires in the area. But it was a sad night for the squadron and for me. Jimmy Begbie, a South African pilot and a great friend was killed. A big man with a tremendous sense of humour and a very easy-going nature it was difficult to believe we shouldn't see him again. The aircraft was attacked by a JU 88 and Jimmy ordered his crew to hit the silk whilst remaining strapped in the aircraft to give the others the opportunity to bale out. Four were successful but Jimmy, his bomb aimer and flight engineer who would have been the last to leave in any event were unable to get out in time and were killed — 'Greater love hath no man'. 'U' for Uncle also failed to return.

And then, to my great dismay, it was Gelsenkirchen in daylight. I think their biggest output in the war was flak and it is most discouraging in daylight, you not only see the stuff but aircraft going down as well. That day was no different, but as we started our run in, the bombsight went unserviceable and there was certainly no time to try and trace the fault, so like the Yanks we dropped our bombs when we saw everyone else dropping theirs. There was a lot of smoke and cloud cover enveloping the target so we were unable to assess the accuracy.

Thankfully, a mining trip came up next, Frederikshavn, just round the most northerly tip of Denmark, in the Kattegat, scene of the Battle of Jutland in the First World War. The weather was lousy and we were treated to a fair share of electrical storms but there was no flak-infested countryside to battle through. We took our datum point from Skagen, the most northerly tip of the Denmark peninsula and did a timed run from there. Incidentally we didn't carry mines with spikes as in the popular films, just about to bounce on the side of a ship until someone pushes it away. Our mines were cylinders and it was all cloaked in mystery because we were told nothing of the weight or the depth at which they would detonate. All the jiggery-pokery was done by a naval officer in the afternoon preceding the raid who calibrated all the settings. I have no idea if they had any potential danger to the aircraft in the case of a prang. After doing our timed run, with no interference at all, I gave the Skipper a new course for home. For the first time on our tour I made a very serious mistake. Lulled by the feeling of a job well done I relaxed, the engines were running with the synchronized beat of a metronome. I was watching the H2S screen and saw the image of a small town coming up. My first reaction was to give a course alteration but on second thoughts I decided not to do anything. I was proved disastrously wrong, a whole basinful of flak came vomiting up. Although I accepted the blame at the time, I cannot recall any warning from intelligence. In retrospect I should have realized that the number of populated areas in Denmark were very limited and if a blip came up on the screen, it should have been given a wide berth. In fact the town was Alborg and what is more housed probably the biggest airfield in Denmark and was literally crawling with 110s. Thank the Lord we were only sent out in foul weather. A dodgy experience, it was good to feel the green, green grass of home once again. I returned a subdued but wiser navigator.

The next two items scheduled for us on the operations board were a disaster. On November eighteenth we were climbing to our operational height *en route* to Munster on the Dortmund-Ems canal when the port outer caught fire after half an hour's flying, and though we had no great problem in dowsing it our chances of reaching the target were remote so we had to abort, and Colin jettisoned the bombs safe about a hundred miles off the east coast. Ten days later our luck ran out again when we should have made our second trip to Essen but with no oil pressure in the port inner engine we never got out of dispersal.

On the last day of the month we were working again and hopefully throwing off our jinx, as we made our second visit to Duisburg. Thankfully as an operational trip it was a non event as there was no fighter activity, searchlights could not penetrate the ten-tenths cloud cover and we were very much in the hands of the Pathfinder boys. In normal circumstances I should explain that we were under the orders and aegis of the élite of Bomber Command, the Master Bombers of the Pathfinder Force. Various devices were used for marking targets, all with weird sounding names — Wanganui, marking with sky markers; Newhaven — marking using H2S and backing up visually; Oboe — marking emanating from home stations using radio transmissions, the markers being released at the point of intersection; Paramatta — which was the code name for ground marking. Whatever was used, I have never been so thrilled as in those few tense minutes over the target to hear the reassuring, precise, unruffled voice of the Master Bomber — "Bomb the Red T.I.s, the greens are spoofs — aim for the ladies' loo on the railway station." Fantastic people, all of whom had completed a tour before volunteering for Pathfinders. On the run in to the dropping point, it was my duty to fuse all the bombs by depressing switches on a board behind me, logging the time and thinking if I am looking at this Omega in ten minutes time, we shall still be alive. But these Pathfinder types orbited the target for anything from ten minutes to half an hour, directing the attack. No praise is too great for people of their calibre. If you were a fighter pilot, you made your decisions by reflex action like an ace tennis player or a cricketer but these people like a professional golfer taking a deciding putt had to be ice cold and completely nerveless.

Soest in north-west Germany was the next nocturnal target for our attention and was a six and a half hour long all round trip to disrupt the marshalling yards and industrial plant. The attack was highly successful and with the flak bursting eighteen thousand feet we climbed to twenty-one thousand, the highest we had ever bombed from and the furthest we had to fall. There was fighter activity both running in and out of the target but nobody was attacked in our wave, although the fighter flares proved a distraction. We touched down at five minutes to eight in the evening having completed approximately half a tour.

We did not have much of a rest as we were on the trail again next night, this time to Osnabruck in north-west Germany, another ancient industrial town situated on a branch of the Mittelland Canal and a strategic rail and road centre. The weather was putrid with heavy cloud and bags of static and, although no markers were seen, the target was easily identified on Gee and combining this with the glow through the clouds, our bombs must have been spot on. As always the flak over the dropping area was concentrated but otherwise we had no trouble, as the immediate area and the flight path back were devoid of populated industrial sites.

Fog in the Vale of York curtailed operations somewhat in December, this part of Yorkshire being prone to a reversal of the adiabetic lapse rate which, put clumsily in layman's terms, meant that contrary to the normal fall in temperature relative to height, the reverse takes place and the heavy air sinks to the ground and condenses out as fog. However we did manage to get aloft on the twenty-first to lay mines in the Kattegat, which was a favourite target area not only because of enemy shipping using the route extensively but it was also a training ground for U-boat crews. Most aircrew liked to go on mining trips because the chance of meeting a fighter was infinitesimal and this night was no exception, no problems at all with the opposition, but the mere fact that over a thousand miles of sea there and back was involved made it no panacea target for me. The rest of the crew must have been bored rigid but I was always tensed up on the way out as the Gee packed up so early, and if the H2S went on the blink, heaven knows where you might finish up, even there if you're lucky. The fog closed in again at Pocklington and we were diverted to Driffield and had to kick our heels at ten o'clock at night waiting for the MT. We couldn't even buy a drink as we were not allowed to take any money with us on ops.

Christmas Eve was another routine day, we were briefed to prang the airfield at Mulheim in the heart of the Ruhr, a target which had a special appeal because it was used by fighters to attack the bomber stream. We took off at seven minutes to one and encountered no opposition until about a hundred miles from the target. I was seated happily tidying up my chart and log, which was a bit of a fetish with me as I liked it to be neat, and such fastidiousness was a great help to maintain a calm mental equilibrium. I was also thinking of the party we should be having that night in the Mess when

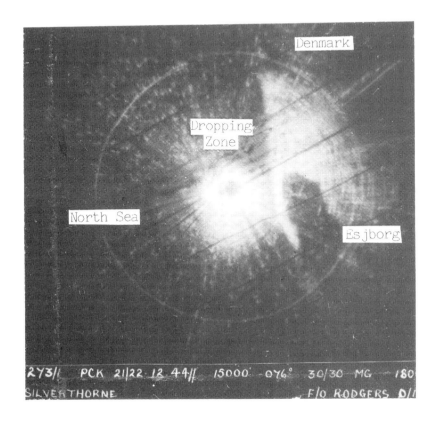

Minelaying off the western coast of Denmark on the night of 21 December, 1944. Photograph taken from a height of 15,000 feet on a true heading of 076 degrees. Navigator F/O Rodgers, aircraft 'D' Dog, 102 Squadron.

the Skipper called over the intercom "Wizzo" (my nickname on the squadron) "come up and have a look at this."

I went up and quite involuntarily blurted out, "Oh Christ!" I had never blasphemed before but I have never stopped using the expression since that day.

Stretching ahead was just a carpet of flak. There is an old lineshoot amongst bomber crews — it was so thick you could have walked on it. We had no option but to fly through it, the stuff was bursting all round and at different heights, and we were holed in several places. It was very clear over the target and we had no problem in picking out the airfield, there was no need to use the target indicators, and Colin dropped our bombs visually. We turned for home still being chased by the flak but escaped without further incident. Fog however had been at work again and closed in base, so we were diverted to Carnaby near Bridlington. And what a shambles! There must have been a third of the main force there, everybody trying to contact their own station. We should have landed at Pocklington at half-past five but it was nearer nine o'clock before we were able to make telephone contact. Later I learnt we had been presumed missing but nobody would go and tell my wife until it was confirmed.

As soon as the news filtered through that we were OK, some be-winged wonder escorted her to the Mess where I joined her much later on to enjoy a very riotous and uninhibited evening. I was not surprised in view of our own experience to learn next day that two of the squadron failed to return.

Koblenz situated at the confluence of the Rhine and the Moselle was our next night objective, a former Roman site, famous for its wines and pianos, surely both go together forging a common denominator with aircrew. It was also the birthplace of Metternich, probably the greatest of all German foreign ministers. From our point of view it was a 'sinecure' trip, literally without care, situated to the east of the Ardennes; it presented no problems with built-up areas and, compared to going to the Ruhr, it was almost a holiday jaunt. Although there was some thin stratus over the target area we had no trouble in locating our objective; the rivers were a giveaway and although the flak was intense and accurate in the area, it was nothing compared to the Ruhr but marked another trip under our belt.

New Year's Eve was another hell-raising night in the Mess and I think it was a miserable gesture of goodwill to stick us on an op on the first day of the New Year. Fortunately we didn't take off until five in the evening so there was plenty of time to shake off the hangover. The aiming point was the railway yards at Dortmund which was situated at the back of the Ruhr and a focal point of the Dortmund-Ems canal. The ack-ack crews must have had a

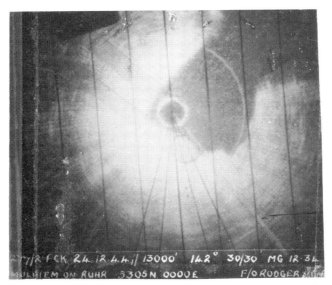

Christmas Eve 1944. H2S photo crossing the Wash on the way to bomb the airfield at Mulheim . . .

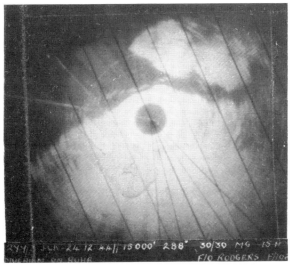

. . . and on the way home from Mulheim. H2S photo taken at 15,000 feet. We are approaching the Belgian coast with the River Scheldt on our starboard

similar night to ourselves, as the opposition was nothing like the normal reception we received from the Ruhr. Although we had no casualties on the op, the return was marred when a pilot on his final approach, undershot the runway, taking the top off a cottage. His bomb aimer was killed and he was severely injured. Next day, a Halifax overshot the runway but nobody was injured. So it was not always over Germany that you were most at risk. Fatigue and tension could induce a lack of concentration and it is remarkable that there were not more accidents of this nature.

We were on again the next night and this was especially significant because it was to be Gerry's (Pilot) last trip before being screened (finished) as he had already done a tour in the Middle East as a gunner. The target they chose for him was Ludwigshafen-Manheim. These were two distinct locations in close proximity, I suppose the hierarchy thought if we didn't hit one we should hit the other, but that is being bloody minded as I am sure we had distinct aiming points. They were situated on the lower reaches of the Rhine and housed the famous I.G. Farbenhindustrie chemical plant and, as with many other German cities, Mannheim had been a cultural centre of Europe because of its association with Mozart.

But thoughts of the *Marriage of Figaro* were far from my thoughts that night as the wind velocity was strong and I had to put more than my usual trust in the accuracy of my navigation.

To make matters worse Gerry was distinctly edgy and kept saying to Colin, the bomb aimer, "Bomb doors open?" And back would come the reply "No." We were now on the last leg and had a hundred mile haul into the target, flying almost due north with the wind gusting from the same direction, and whilst we were not exactly stationary it must have been the slowest progress we had ever made on our tour. Another enquiry of Colin brought back the response, "I haven't come all this bloody way to drop the bombs in a field." Over the target, visibility was good and we bombed the Pathfinders' markers and I talked Gerry into turning rapidly into the right direction because I knew that once out of the danger area we had a reasonably clear run for home. This was accomplished without any undue scares but it was somewhat ironic that the longest trip we had ever done, seven and a half hours, should coincide with Gerry's last operational trip over the Third Reich.

This was the end of a long association, Gerry had seen us through a maelstrom of difficult situations and never once did I know him to panic. We had known our differences, there is no pilot breathing that flies meticulously the courses his navigator feeds him, but there must exist a mutual trust and confidence between the two and experience had forged that link. So it was over bar the farewells, which were exchanged at a party in the local pub which Gerry gave for us and our faithful groundcrew. A month after finishing, his Distinguished Flying Cross came through by which time he had left the station and I never ever saw him again.

Ronnie Heiden, another South African pilot who was at the party and one of our closest friends went missing with his crew, two nights later over Hanover, the third to go out of the original eight Springboks. We had a respite from flying whilst waiting for our new Skipper to arrive but there were several days of snow when no one was airborne. About the middle of the month, operations started again and one of the first casualties was Squadron Leader Jarand, officer commanding 'C' Flight a regular of ineffable charm. He was good company and had an idiosyncrasy of swilling his beer round his pint pot which will always stick in my memory. He had been a good friend of mine and was one of those types you looked on as indestructible.

Towards the end of the month, our new Skipper arrived Flight Lieutenant Maurice Bennett who had already done one tour. Funnily enough he had been our instructor at 1664 Heavy Conversion Unit at Dishforth and he was one of the fraternity who had voted our crew as a poor survival risk, probably because of the navigator. So I don't think he could have been too enamoured at the thought of being crewed up with us.

The first of February saw us dicing again with our new Skipper bound for Mainz, capital of the Rhine Palatinate and a former Roman town, another inland port situated on the Rhine on the opposite side to Wiesbaden and thirty-five miles south-west of Frankfurt, a strategic port of communications. Apart from being another long haul, the trip was uneventful, the flak was bursting below our height, there was 10/10ths cloud over the target and with no searchlight problems we bombed the red target indicators visible over the glow of the fires.

Two nights later we went mining to Cuxhaven and as we were approaching the dropping area I forgot to tell the Skipper to open the bomb doors which must have confirmed his first impressions of the crew's capabilities. So we had to go round again and this time we were greeted with a barrage of flak over Cuxhaven itself, but having sown our vegetables we had another uneventful slog home.

Another long trip, four nights later, took us to Goch which was believed to be full of German troops, but the whole trip was a fiasco from the squadron point of view. We had to abandon the mission on the Master Bomber's instructions, a lot of effort for nothing. The flak was heavy and the fighter boys were mixing it, one pilot who was shot down left his RT on

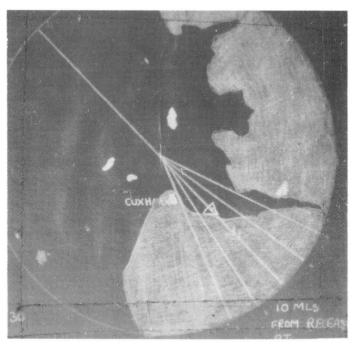

H2S mock-up of minelaying trip at the mouth of the Elbe

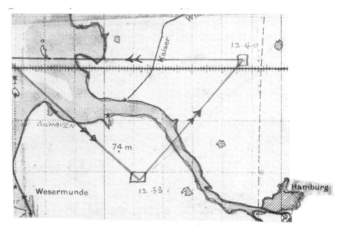

Navigator's chart showing route into the dropping point and, what is more important, the way out

and you could hear his screams. We lost two aircraft out of seventeen but all the crew of one baled out with the exception of the pilot. We jettisoned our bombs over the sea.

On February 13th we were briefed for Leipzig which was at the junction of four main railway lines. Its importance at this period of the war was its proximity to the Russian advance and, as Churchill had promised to give Allied air support, this raid was to be one of those gestures. One of Leipzig's sons typified the spirit of Germany with his music of empirical splendour, his name was Richard Wagner. It was here also that Johann Sebastian Bach wrote some of his major compositions. Of such stuff were the traditions of this ancient town of Saxony. Such culture about to be laid waste, but we never got there. It was a bizarre occasion, after briefing we were issued with a placard to be worn round our necks like a child evacuee, on one side was the Union Jack and on the reverse written in Russian were words to the effect 'I am a British Airman'. One of the intelligence bods called me aside after the briefing and said, "For Christ's sake don't bale out over the target area." I realized the implication but all four engines would have had to drop off before I hit the silk. I almost changed my mind after we had been airborne for upwards of an hour.

I was busy on my chart when suddenly the aircraft started to vibrate and for a moment we were completely at a loss to know what had happened, but after what seemed an interminable delay, the Skipper and engineer diagnosed a runaway propellor. The problem of overspeeding in an engine is not normally a cause for alarm but this went right off the clock and there was a distinct possibility of dislodging the engine mounting. The procedure to rectify the fault is beyond the ken of a mere navigator to know. I believe it was policy to neutralize the identical engine on the other side. Sufficient to say, the remedy took too long for comfort and I have been frightened far less over Germany than I was at this mishap. Sufficient to say it was a very shaky effort, but with a Skipper of our calibre and an engineer, we were in very capable hands but I was more than a happy little navigator when the wheels hit the tarmac.

Our luck seemed to have run out as the very next night we were on the board for a gardening trip but after all the preliminaries of running up engines, testing equipment and consultations with the ground crew, we had to admit defeat as the port inner wouldn't function. As our tour was now well advanced, losing a plum op was a big disappointment.

On the twenty-seventh of February we returned to Mainz to finish the job we started on the first, which was to destroy the rail communications and the adjoining buildings. We were now flying the Halifax VI which did not make any difference as far as I was concerned, but technically the Hercules engines were stronger and the aircraft had a greater range. The attack again was an unqualified success and although we had fighter cover, they were never needed. The flak was innocuous and one gained the impression that isolated targets were not as well defended as before.

The second of March saw the end of Cologne when six hundred bombers made a daylight raid on the city in order to neutralize the approaches to the Rhine crossings. We were in the last wave of the attack and the sight was quite unbelievable. The ack-ack was completely negligible and we circled the Cathedral which stood out in an area of total devastation, like a sore thumb on a moon landscape. How it escaped must be one of the wonders of the war; although it was pock-marked with shrapnel, the structure itself stood out like a symbol and if I had been a religious person, I would have attributed this miracle to divine providence. We had a grand-stand view of the Rhine and some spectacular fires were engulfing warehouses along its banks. Again, fighters were conspicuous by their absence and was further confirmation that the defences were cracking.

On the following night we went to Kamen, another oil producing target and the home of the Fischer-Tropsch plant. This was another six hour trip which produced no fireworks until we returned to base. I should point out that once we had crossed the enemy or occupied coast on the return journey our feelings with the dangers behind us were at a pinnacle of euphoria. In fact, I have never since experienced a feeling of such depth.

In between giving the Skipper the odd fix, I used to sing all the way back, with the microphone switched off of course, but this night was to be the last time. Normally, I liked to be one of the first back and on this particular night it proved most fortuitous. We had just turned off the main runway and I threw open the astrodome for some fresh air when I happened to glance back and saw tracer pouring into a Halifax. I shouted to the Skipper and he turned off at the end of the runway and parked on the grass, switched off the navigation lights, cut the engines and we all clambered out and ran like hell across the airfield. I saw three Halifaxes shot down, huge balls of fire when they hit the deck. We tore across to the de-briefing but this was abandoned as the Jagdgeschwader were still flying over the airfield. Apparently JU 88s and 188s had followed the 4 Group bomber stream all the way back from Germany and picked the psychological moment to attack. Returning from a raid, the air space above the closely sited airfields was something akin to spaghetti junction with bombers first being directed into an outer ring system which served roughly three airfields before being called into their own circuit. So it was a kaleidoscope of red green and white

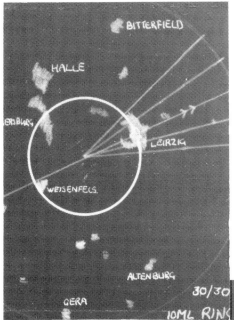

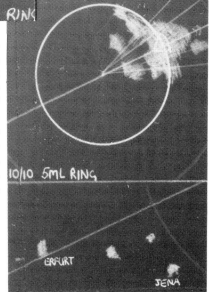

First illustration of an H2S mock-up of the attack on Leipzig which we aborted. The response from Leipzig would first appear on the right hand edge of the screen, and to drop the bombs we would track down the line with the two arrows until the circle cut the city. By means of a switch we transferred to a larger picture and when the circle cut the town, we dropped the bombs.

lights acting as homing beams to the attackers. It was chaos as airfield lights were switched off and diversions were ordered to other stations but some just ran out of fuel before they could find sanctuary. It was an unprecedented situation, one which had never been envisaged at this state of the war. There was no future in hanging about the drome and I made my way down to the cottage but not before throwing myself into the hedge when a Junkers 88 flew over my head with a deafening roar from the BMW radial engines. I reached the cottage, somewhat out of breath to find my wife, the landlady and the baby huddled in the passage, they had heard the tremendous racket going on but fortunately no houses were strafed, Halifaxes were the sole target.

Little was heard officially of this raid and the only source I have seen spoke of seventy of the two hundred and ten who attacked Kamen were either shot down or crashed through lack of fuel, and this was against Luftwaffe fighter casualties of seven out of seventy who made the attack. I cannot believe that the losses were of such magnitude but my impression was that there was an inordinate number of casualties in 4 Group and losses percentage wise must have been well in excess of the norm acceptable for an operation. Whatever happened was a well kept secret; nothing filtered through from the intelligence section and I am pretty certain that the hierarchy played it down for fear that the news of the marauders' success reaching the enemy would invite a return visit. But you can't censor the talk amongst aircrews in their cups, and Betty's Bar was the setting for many a lurid account of the happenings on the night of March the third.

After Kamen, we were very jumpy on the home stretch, and flying six trips in twenty days didn't help the situation. We were lucky in having a superb pilot. One late afternoon returning from a daylight, the visibility over base clamped to around three hundred to four hundred yards and no aircraft had landed. Eventually, flying control asked Maurice to give it a stab and remark on the possibility of talking down the other crews. This in effect was an acknowledgement that he was one of the best pilots on the squadron. We made it through the murk and Maurice radioed control that he would not advise any other aircraft to try it. Another night when we were returning across the North Sea, Jerry dropped a line of flares like a Guy Fawkes night display of pyrotechnics. When we were tucking into our bacon and egg afterwards I told him he had done a hell of a good job. His reply was, "Don't thank me, thank George!" (the automatic pilot).

On another daylight we took off in conditions close on fog, this was one of those days when Group were determined to get us off the deck. In order to do this, flying control posted a bod half-way down the runway and as each

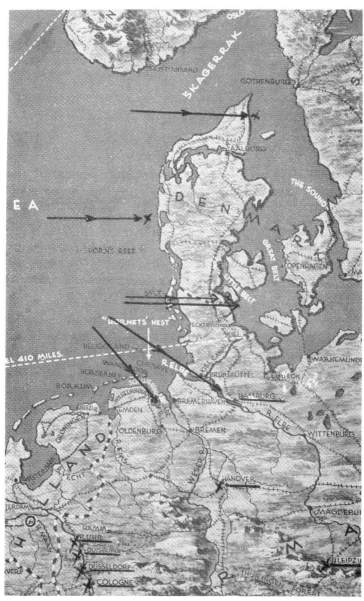

Minelaying in the Kattegat and the North Sea (arrowed) and some bombing targets in the Ruhr

kite went past him in the mist, he gave the all clear to the next aircraft by R/T. Having left the secure bosom of Mother Earth, one climbed through the overcast into brilliant sunshine and another daylight was on the way. I used to set course from York Minster which was a matter of minutes from the airfield, whilst 5 Group who flew Lancasters used Lincoln Cathedral, so at least we started off with the benefit of the Church.

Karl-Marx-Stadt may sound an unusual target, but this is the name now given by the Russians to the former city of Chemnitz which we were due to attack on the night of March fifth, to implement the promises made to the Russians at Yalta to mount air attacks on communications and troop movements on the eastern front.

Unfortunately, a hundred miles out over the North Sea, the gremlins struck and the port outer packed up. Since we could not make the operational height or maintain the necessary airspeed it would have been suicide to press on, as Chemnitz was approximately thirteen degrees east. So I logged our position and at just over four thousand feet jettisoned the load safe.

Two nights later, we were back on the horticultural run planting vegetables (mines) off the Flensburg Fjord and in the waters of Kiel Bay. We had a trouble free trip but one aircraft went down in the target area and another in the sea on the homeward trip. The aircraft could either have flown over a flak ship which would have been decidedly unlucky or picked off by a night fighter. Either way, it was proof that these trips were not always the piece of cake one expected them to be.

The following night we were out again in a combined bombing and mine laying expedition centred on Hamburg and we were the horticultural experts. For the first and last time we dropped our mines on sky markers and the defences, for a change, were as innocuous as a shower in the Sahara. Still it was another one for the log-book, and with only six more to go we were within striking distance of the finishing tape.

The adrenalin started working again when another daylight target came up in the shape of Wuppertal, which stood on a tributary of the Rhine and was really ersatz, as it embraced several smaller towns and received its overall title from the fact that the common factor was the river Wupper. At this stage in the war, the opposition had become academic, although one had to respect the flak in the target area, and there was always the chance an unlucky shell could be yours. We had a strong fighter cover who were not called into action but it was a very comforting sight to see them several thousand feet above you. Again the flak was sporadic and we had an almost free ride into the target area, where we bombed the blue smoke puffs, as

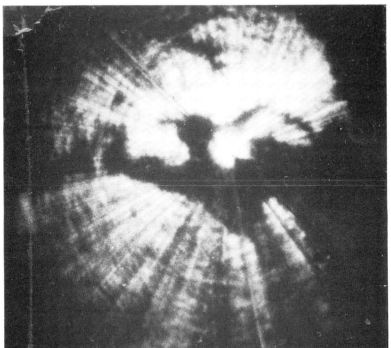

395. PCK. 7/8·3·45//(B) FLENSBURG FIORD F/O. RODGERS F/102
1. 10000'. 175T. 30/20. 21·57. 263 $^{54.32N}_{1003E}$ 8½

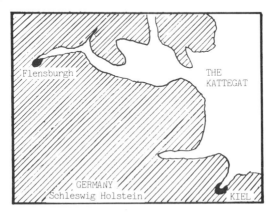

Laying Mines at Flensburg Fiord 7th and 8th March, 1945. Map shows the area in which the mines were laid

ten-tenths cloud covered the aiming points.

March the fourteenth saw us bound for Homburg to block road and rail routes and destroy enemy armour and troops. We went in at twelve thousand feet which was probably the lowest we had ever bombed, earlier in the tour we would have been a flying colander but today there was no particular difficulty, and although the ground was covered in a slight haze the markers appeared to be spot on.

Our last daylight was a return visit to Osnabruck and we were airborne before seven o'clock in the morning with the intended object of bombing industrial plant and disrupting communications. Over the Continent we were joined by an impressive fighter cover, a lovely sight on a spring morning. So much for Goering's boast that no enemy aircraft would fly over the Third Reich. The flak over the target was quite heavy and accurate but this did not deter us from bombing visually through gaps in the stratus. A very self-satisfied crew winged its way home and were sinking pints when we heard the one o'clock news.

At one time it was a relief when your name did not appear on the operations board but now we were keen to finish. However, ten days elapsed before we were out again when we were called on to destroy the repaired and partly active oil refinery at Harburg. We had a quiet trip and after we had bombed, we saw three large explosions in the target area and fires were visible up to fifteen miles away.

The penultimate trip, again at night, was Hamburg and the object was to destroy naval installations, shipyard buildings, prefabricated submarines, and concentrations of shipping. There was 9/10ths cloud over the target and we bombed the markers from twenty thousand feet. Again we had no trouble with the defences. We were second home, beaten by six minutes, although the winners had a three minute start on us.

We were not kept in suspense very long waiting for the final trip to come up because we were on again the next night, back to the old stamping ground of Flensburg. Couldn't have been a better one, at least one hoped so. It certainly was a very different kettle of fish to Gerry's last on Ludwigshafen.

I unfolded my Mercator chart for the last time, odd to ponder that Gerardus Mercator almost four hundred years ago translated the latitudes and longitudes from the curves of the globe to the straight lines and right angles which constituted my chart. I checked the other navigation aids and found them to be in perfect nick, and after the usual cockpit preliminaries we were once again airborne — but now for the last time. I must confess to having a few butterflies in the stomach, many a crew bought it on their last trip. But I need have had no fears, it was a perfect trip, a spot on landfall and what was quite remarkable and had never happened before, we never saw one burst of flak. There are no prizes for guessing who was the first back, we won by several lengths. It was probably the easiest operation we had ever experienced. We taxied to our usual dispersal on the Pocklington road and climbed out to enjoy the usual whistle which was sheer heaven after being stuck in 'Fanny By Searchlight' for nearly five hours. Then came the most emotional moment of my life; one member of the crew came up and said, "Thanks for seeing us through Wizzo," and we all shook hands, very much close to tears. We had been on operations for some eight months, we had experienced our ups and downs both literally and metaphorically, but now at last we were on cloud nine.

6

CHAIRBORNE (MARK II)

A couple of days later, Phil Morris called me into the Navigation Leader's office and showed me my citation for a DFC. In point of fact, it never came through and I was naturally disappointed. It may have been because I turned down the suggestion of another operational tour in the Far East. The actual project put to me was the dropping of supplies at low level from a Dakota over the jungles of Burma. This hardly had me jumping for joy especially as I had only just started my statutory six months rest from dicing with death over the Third Reich. My wife was in a most interesting condition, *en ventre sa mere*, and I was not exactly suffering any withdrawal symptoms from operational flying.

I should point out that the DFC could be an immediate award for some exceptional flying feat on operations and not many of these were awarded, only one to my knowledge whilst I was operating and that was to a South African. Alternatively, it was usually awarded to the pilot and navigator who survived a reasonable tour. This was more or less standard procedure in the latter days of the war. But I felt very sorry for one of my colleagues, Peter Roscoe, a chartered accountant and a regular officer who gave up a safe post as an Accountant Officer and dropped a rank in order to fly, he was also passed by. Fortunately, he soldiered on, which is a paradox in terms to become ultimately an Air Commodore and was rewarded with the insignia of the Commander of the Bath, one of the highest accolades it is possible to be awarded in a service career.

In retrospect, I think a gong for the pilot was well merited, no Skipper could negotiate a tour without displaying great skill and courage, besides the onus of carrying the responsibility, in fair weather and foul, through thick and thin, the lives of six other crew members. Like the long distance runner, it took a lot of guts to see it through. I have reservations about the navigator's entitlement to recognition. Navigation was the most time-consuming job in the aircraft, life centred around the chart, the log, the green fluorescent images of the Gee set and the silver-grey rebounds on the H2S. You were cocooned in your own little world, cushioned from the outside dangers by the need for constant calculation. Not so the poor

Airmen's memorial, York Minster

gunners, there is no way I would have flown in their position, virtually isolated, searching the blackness for hour after hour, alleviated only by moments of real fear when the action started and the flak burst all around.

The chief reward of any aircrew however was survival and carping about the merits and demerits of gongs are trivia. But accepting this, Bomber Command aircrew were deliberately slighted by the powers that be by their failure to issue a campaign medal. All aircrew would have been happy to have a Bomber Command Star or an extension of the Aircrew Europe, but after the war, many politicians and others no longer wished to be associated with the Command of which the bombing of Dresden could have been the flashpoint.

It is not for the minnows of Bomber Command like myself to offer judgements on the controversial circumstances surrounding the bombing of Dresden, but as certain as this city was literally destroyed overnight, Bomber Command metaphorically suffered the same fate. The whole affair was a catastrophe of gargantuan proportions. As to why it took place and who in the final judgement was responsible, no one will ever really know. But even so, it has been taken out of context, we were at war and war is total. At the time of the attack, we were committed to give the Russians, who were in close proximity, every possible military assistance. If it had happened in 1940 or 1941 there would not have been an outcry of comparable magnitude. And one might reflect on what would have been the fate of cities like Exeter, Bath, and many others, if the bombers' role had been reversed.

Unfortunately, the moralists, the do-gooders, the critics, the reneguers, were provided with a weapon to aggravate a self-inflicted wound. The breed of people at home who drew comfort from the fact that the war was prosecuted against the heart of the enemy by the bomber crews when the tide of war was running very much against us is fast dying away. So it is fitting to remind the critics that more than half of all aircrew who flew on Bomber Command operations were killed and a further eighteen thousand were wounded or taken prisoner of war. An unprecedented five thousand lost their lives in training alone besides the countless injured.

Naturally, surviving aircrew are particularly sensitive to the post-war criticism of Bomber Command and to the cavalier treatment of one of the great architects of victory, Marshal of the Royal Air Force, Sir Arthur T. Harris, 'Bomber' to his boys.

A week after finishing ops, we were chosen to accept on behalf of the Royal Air Force, the last Halifax bomber, *London Pride*, built by the London Passenger Transport Board. The ceremony took place at Leavesden Aerodrome so we travelled to London and were taken out to

Unveiling ceremony of the last Halifax bomber London Pride, built by the London Passenger Transport Board — 16 April, 1945

Taking off in London Pride from Leavesden Aerodrome — our last trip in a last Halifax bomber, 16 April 1945

lunch and thence to the airfield. There we met Lord Ashfield, Chairman of the LPTB and Sir Frederick Handley Page, one of the giants in aviation history.

The proceedings were attended by many of the board's employees, besides RAF bigwigs and reputedly the Gaumont News, but I can't say I ever saw any recording although we were subsequently presented with a portfolio of photographs of the occasion, including airborne shots.

The aircraft was in a large hangar and it was surprising how much bigger it appeared in a confined space after being used to see it only in the open air. A Union Jack covered the name and coat of arms emblazoned on the side of the aircraft below the cockpit, and this was duly unveiled by Lord Ashfield who paid a well deserved tribute to the work force responsible for building two hundred of these superb aircraft.

We then climbed into *London Pride* (for the record, number PN 460 of aircraft contract ACFT 2595) and were joined by the Group Chief Test Pilot, T. W. Morton. This was a finale in more ways than one, the last Halifax to be built by the Board and for us the last time we flew in a Halifax together. It certainly was a never-to-be-forgotten experience. The standard operational procedure was to run up the engines, throttle back, release the brakes and advance the throttles as the speed increased. But this was no time for going by the book, T. W. M. probably helped to write it anyway. Throttles advanced to the gate, we were airborne like a Spitfire and this 'Supremo' of the stick proceeded to give an unbelievable display of aerobatics, feathering engines in all sorts of permutations and roaring over the airstrip at zero feet, it must have been an awe-inspiring sight from the spectators' point of view.

We touched down at White Waltham, signed the acceptance certificate, and were whisked away to the Metropolis and the hospitality of the Strand Palace Hotel. Here, we were joined by some charming female companions from the company with whom we danced the night away. The London Passenger Transport Board had given us a fabulous time and we were very grateful. For Maurice, it was a signal honour to be chosen from all the pilots in the Group and confirmed the high regard in which he was held.

Our return to Pocklington was something of an anticlimax, no longer part of the operational scene, there was none of the original crowd of South Africans left and, although Maurice and I had been earlier promised a cushy job of air testing Halifaxes, we never got the job due to administrative changes in the squadron hierarchy. So it was a very sad day when we were all posted to different stations. Maurice was awarded a bar to his DFC, a well merited honour. He was one of only two persons ever to be awarded a bar whilst serving on 102 squadron.

I was posted to Breighton as a spare navigator but I only flew once, taking a sprog crew over France. I told the pilot he could fly anywhere he liked for the next two hours when I would take a Gee fix to take us back to base. I settled down to read a book but after half an hour I looked out and found we were flying down a V-shaped valley with trees framing either side of the aircraft. It was most exhilarating as we continued our odyssey over the French countryside. I let him have his head for a few more minutes and then told him to get some height. I didn't fancy finishing up as a corpse in a French vineyard. We returned to Breighton where he made a real bouncer of a landing.

Then I had a fabulous stroke of luck, I was very friendly with an Irish wing commander and he was instrumental in obtaining an interview for me at 4 Group Headquarters with a view to being a staff officer. I duly presented myself at a stately home, Heslington Hall, now York University, where I was interviewed by the Air Officer Commanding, Air Vice Marshal Sir Hugh Walmsley. I was pretty nervous but, being the gentleman he was, he put me completely at ease, and when he learned I had been articled to a chartered accountant and at that time, they were short of a mess secretary, I was appointed. I was delighted to accept the position which involved other responsibilities such as air sea rescue information being fed out to squadrons in the medium of films. I also prepared reports on the efficiency of squadrons besides doing accountancy investigation work. I had to make enquiries into the loss of parachutes at one station and found they were in great demand for ladies' underwear. My immediate chief was Group Captain A. F. Johnson CBE, DFC who had done most of his operational flying in the Middle East. I did some flights with him in the course of my duties and was most impressed by his capabilities. The Senior Air Staff Officer was Air Commodore 'Gus' Walker who had been such an inspiration to the 4 Group bomber crews. I did several jobs for him, not the least being Christmas Eve when he asked me if I had any ideas for seasonal decorations and was delighted when I had the bright idea of using 'window', the tinfoil strips we dropped to fog the German radar.

It certainly was one of the most pleasant periods of my service life, at lunch-time we used to play a most unusual game of bowls. We bowled from a top lawn which had a one in three fall to the next terraced lawn, we had a standard white jack but the balls weren't round, they were square. The Hall was the former home of Lord Deramore, appropriately a squadron leader who at one time had been stationed in the Hall.

Ninety per cent of the staff at the Group were aircrew officers and I

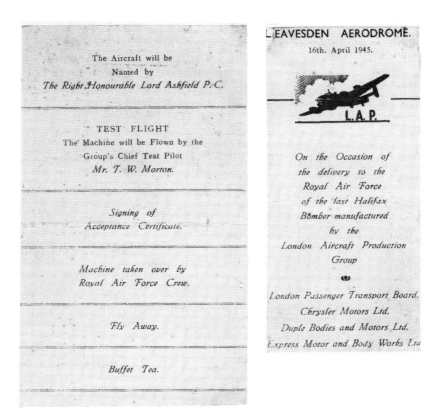

The Aircraft will be
Named by
The Right Honourable Lord Ashfield P.C.

TEST FLIGHT
The Machine will be Flown by the
Group's Chief Test Pilot
Mr. T. W. Morton.

*Signing of
Acceptance Certificate.*

*Machine taken over by
Royal Air Force Crew.*

Fly Away.

Buffet Tea.

LEAVESDEN AERODROME.

16th. April 1945.

L.A.P.

*On the Occasion of
the delivery to the
Royal Air Force
of the last Halifax
Bomber manufactured
by the
London Aircraft Production
Group*

*London Passenger Transport Board,
Chrysler Motors Ltd,
Duple Bodies and Motors Ltd,
Express Motor and Body Works Ltd*

*Official programme to mark the handing-over ceremony of the
last Halifax bomber*

formed a very firm friendship with an air bomber, Alan Washbrook, who was a seasoned operational aircrew member, having made fifteen trips to Berlin. He naturally had a DFC and was expecting a bar. I used to visit the York library to check the *London Gazette* to see if our names were there. I must have been a bit dim in those days or alcohol anaesthetized, because there were sources on the Group who could have enlightened me. We enjoyed some good nights in York, particularly the Half Moon and Betty's Bar, the latter was the time honoured meeting place of all bomber crews. I was billeted with a very nice family at Acomb, husband and wife both Salvation Army members who did enormous good work, but I think they disapproved of the hours I kept. One morning my landlord remonstrated with me for not bolting the front door when I came in. The following evening I dutifully obeyed his instructions and I was somewhat shaken next morning when he came across to me. He was not a swearing man, "Thanks for bolting the front door, but next time, shut the bloody thing first," he said.

In the course of my duties I used to visit several airfields which was a good excuse to look up old 'oppos'. On these jaunts I had the use of a staff Hillman or the luxury of a Dragon Rapide which was stationed at Full Sutton for the use of Heslington Hall types.

A little nostalgia of wartime flying came back in July 1945 when Group Captain Johnson was invited to be guest of honour at an RAF party in Whitchurch. He took me along, advising me not to put up any blacks since I was a staff officer. We picked up an Anson at Full Sutton and in less than two hours touched down. It was a ding-dong of a party and I met a Wren officer whom I had known before the war in Sheffield, but I think the rank had gone to her head as she wasn't keen on making further aquaintance. We took off again next morning at eleven o'clock, which was a bit early after a night out, and we had been flying for about an hour when the weather closed in. The Group Captain was flying visually as it was only a two hour trip. He turned to me and said, "You're the navigator, where the hell are we?" I hadn't a clue as well he knew. We were now down to a few hundred feet despite the maxim 'height is might' when flying, but quite by chance an airstrip appeared out of the gloom and we lobbed down safely at Church Broughton on what was to be my last flight in the RAF. From there we returned by MT to Heslington and 'Johnny' made straight to the operations room to see if there were any problems with training aircraft, borrowed some money from me for cigarettes, which reminds me he still owes me. He was a good friend and boss and it was through him I obtained an extended service commission, since there were no permanent commissions being

June ~ October
1943

⚜ ⚜ ⚜

Souvenir
Menu

Flight Banquet
Course 78
No. 1 Central
Navigation School

Rivers
Manitoba Canada

Oct. 26th. 1943

Official functions — the first . . .

102 (CEYLON) SQUADRON

REUNION
DINNER AND DANCE

Programme

CAFE ROYAL : LONDON
MAY 10th. 1947

. . . and the last

granted at the time and most senior officers were dropping a rank.

Whilst I was at Heslington, I had a queer experience when I was duty officer. I had already been disturbed by a Waaf officer who said there was an airman and a girl in the grounds of the Waafery and what was I going to do about it. Being an ardent supporter of Women's Lib in those days I replied, "Nothing." She said she would put in a report but nothing ever came of it. To get back to the hall. Around two o'clock in the morning I heard footsteps going down the corridor which was about the length of two cricket pitches. I had heard before that the place was haunted and when the footsteps finally faded away I plucked up courage to investigate. I checked two floors and found no sign of anybody; person, animal or other phenomenon. I wonder whether any students have been similarly disturbed since?

Group Captain Johnson had a brainwave to organize a garden party at the hall and I was the dogsbody deputed to make the arrangements. We invited the top brass from all over the country and were fortunate enough to obtain the services of Dan Maskell and some of his contemporaries to give us a tennis exhibition, and although it was unfortunately one of those anti-cyclonic days with an overcast sky and some drizzle, they insisted in carrying on, which I thought was a most commendable gesture.

Only one more anecdote; it was Christmas Eve, about nine o'clock when the Wing Commander Engineering collared me and said, "I have a job for you. The WAAF Squadron Officer wants someone to judge the decorations in the girls' huts and you're just the bloke I am looking for." I made great protestations to no avail and had to trail round these huts with two WAAF officers in attendance, which was most embarrassing as several of the girls had been on night duty and were still in bed. Still it made a welcome change to the previous Christmas Eve over Essen.

In 1946 I was temporarily seconded as assistant accountant officer at Melbourne, the home of 'Shiny' 10. I was not there very long but just before I left some workmen moved in and started replacing panes of glass and painting the huts. As I knew the airfield was to be closed, known technically as on care and maintenance, I rang up the Group to inform them. The reply was that the airfield buildings had to be put in the same position as taken over. I also helped out at Riccall on the accountancy side and spent half my time refusing petrol coupons.

But both Alan Washbrook and myself were getting a bit restless, myself in particular, as the Air Force, not unnaturally, was reverting to its peacetime status. We had several nights on the town with our inseparable companion Squadron Leader Bob Marsh who had won an AFC on the Continent for carrying out confidential work, mostly flying Ansons in very

PARTY TIME

Invitation from the Air Officer Commanding, 4 Group

Farewell party, RAF Pocklington

dicey weather. A certain Wing Commander came out with us one night, at his own request, but half-way through the evening started pulling rank, so he never got the chance to come again.

At the end of the summer, I resigned my commission and I made a last nostalgic trip to Pocklington and received a pleasant surprise. I went into one of the deserted rooms and found the floor was littered with radar and bombing photographs, so I waded through the lot and found as many as I could of my own, and they subsequently found their way into my log-book.

At Group the top AOC job had been downgraded to Air Commodore, and before I went, he asked me to go round the art dealers in York and find a suitable painting for the Mess. I came back with a reproduction Peter Scott depicting wild geese taking off, which I thought was singularly appropriate for a RAF Mess. The Air Commodore was not impressed although the painting was duly hung but, that was not the end of the story. Just before I left, the AOC came up trumps and threw a cocktail party for myself and another officer, in my case, it was probably a thanksgiving at getting rid of me. As a parting shot however, he said, "You can have that Peter Scott," and it is still on my wall to this day.

That was not quite the end of my association with 4 Group. One morning I saw a photograph of Alan in the national papers and I quote from one: 'The bombs are designed to produce such enormous blast that the Valiants will be caught in it unless they escape immediately after the bomb aimer calls out "Bombs Away". By the time the intense flash of the bomb lights up the aircraft cabin, the crew will have to be miles away, if they are to survive. They will only have thirty seconds.' Alan was, of course, the bomb aimer, he must have been a glutton for punishment. The exercise was known as 'Operation Grapple' based on Christmas Island, in the Pacific.

It was of course successful and Alan was awarded the Air Force Cross. I wrote and congratulated him and here is an extract from his letter to me dated the 26th May 1957:

'I was delighted to hear from you again after all these years. It has taken ten years off my age just to sit down and read your letter. It was a very straightforward job for me, can't see the reason for all the ballyhoo. The boffins are the ones who deserve the write-up.'

That marked the end of a saga which started with a bromide laced cup of tea in Warrington, and ended with a cocktail party in York.

7

PERSONALITIES

I was very fortunate that although I was a junior officer with no operational gongs to my credit, I met or rubbed shoulders with some of the people in the hierarchy of Bomber Command.

Air Chief Marshal Sir Augustus Walker GCB, CBE, DSO, DFC, AFC

'Gus' as he was affectionately known throughout Bomber Command was one of the personalities with whom I had most contact, both from a flying point of view and later in my duties attached to his Staff at 4 Group Headquarters, which incidentally, was originally commanded by 'Bomber' Harris.

The career of Sir Augustus, had it been fiction, would have defied credibility. He was a brilliant Rugby player, obtaining a blue at Cambridge and an international cap with England at fly half. He had a very distinguished operational record which went back as far as 1941 when he was a Flight Commander on Hampdens. After successful tours he received a grave injury when he lost his right arm running to warn a Lancaster crew, from whose bomb bays incendiaries had fallen. He was within twenty yards of the aircraft when the 'cookie' went off with disastrous consequences. But symbolic of his character, and I quote the late Guy Gibson, another flyer of epic stature — 'Before he was taken to base hospital, he said two things. He asked me if I would look for his arm, which had a brand new glove on it and he told me to ring up the AOC and asked him if he would take on a one-armed Station Commander.'

Whilst I was operating, he was Base Commander, a job which was no sinecure and a position which he took very seriously. He made a point of attending take offs and landings at the stations under his command. The aircrews were a mixed bag of Australians, Canadians, South Africans, and us 'Pommies', and his popularity was universal. His outstanding characteristic was his ability to mix with all ranks in which he excelled. It was indeed a privilege to become one of his personal staff in what was the happiest period of my service career.

After the war, he became Deputy Commander in Chief, Allied Forces,

Central Europe. But one of the honours which must have afforded him a great amount of pleasure was to be elected President of the Rugby Football Union.

He still sends his regards through a mutual Exmouth friend, Archie Dymond who sees him regularly at 'Twickers'.

Wing Commander Guy Gibson VC, DSO, DFC

Guy Gibson, the legendar hero of 617 Squadron, the Dam Busters, came to Rivers (Canada) shortly after the raid and gave us a graphic account of the operation and what life was like in Bomber Command. He also paid great tribute to the American Eighth Air Force. To see a hero like Gibson in the flesh was a tremendous tonic and spur to us lesser mortals, stuck out in the prairie, grappling with the mysteries and intricacies of navigation.

Group Captain D. O. Young DSO, DFC, AFC

That above was the Commanding Officer at Pocklington during my tour. As such he was responsible for the running of the whole station but the operational flying side fell to a great extent on his immediate subordinate, the Wing Commander in charge of the squadron. Group Captain Young had a distinguished flying career which was prefaced by thousands of hours of civilian flying. He was operational when the going was really hard. Normally aircrews did not have very much contact with the Station CO either socially or disciplinary. My contacts bordered on the disastrous. On the first occasion he indicated in no mild manner that my presence in the Mess (after closing time) was surplus to requirements when he caught me chatting up a Waaf waitress.

The second time, I was more sinned against than sinning and it was certainly not my fault but undoubtedly due to my South African colleagues. We had imbibed a few pints in a very convivial night in the Feathers and the party included my wife. There were no ops scheduled for next day and against my better judgement we were shanghaied into the Mess. Females were allowed into the hallowed quarters on only two nights a week and this wasn't one of them. I pointed out the dangers very strongly but arguing with a bunch of colonials is like trying to roll back the tide. So we went back and as luck would have it the CO dropped in for a nightcap. Next day I was collared by the PMC who read the riot act, not that it sunk very deeply. It was hardly a hanging affair but I thought it prudent not to tell my South African colleagues, or we could have had an international incident.

Wilf Bickley CGM

Although our paths never crossed during the war, I first met Wilf in 1950 when I made Exmouth my home. I have dedicated my story to him because he epitomizes the real operational type. People like myself made a fleeting impression on the scene, but men of his calibre were the real professionals and undoubtedly the heroes of Bomber Command.

In all he flew ninety trips and was awarded the CGM after 71. After the VC this award is the most coveted and highly prestigious decoration which could be earned on aircrew operations. As a tail gunner, he was cut off from the rest of the crew and spent many long hours scanning an alien sky, sometimes in sub zero temperatures, but kept awake by the knowledge that the lives of the whole crew were dependent on his vigilance. He graduated from Hampdens in the early days to the Lancasters of the never to be forgotten 617 Squadron. He flew on two raids on the *Tirpitz* skulking in a Norwegian fiord and the classic raid of the war, the Dam Busters from which only half the crews retured.

The last paragraph in his citation for the CGM says it all: 'This Warrant Officer has an outstanding operational record. He has invariably shown irrepressible courage and fighting spirit. He is a man who is undaunted by the heaviest defences and who can be depended upon to overcome the strongest opposition. His great gallantry and superb fighting qualities have always been in keeping with the highest traditions of the Service and he is therefore strongly recommended for the immediate award of the CGM.'

Group Captain Leonard Cheshire VC, OM, DSO, DFC

In 1948, we had a squadron reunion at the Café Royale and the above was one of the Guests of Honour. I had no idea who he was when he came into the banqueting hall but he had an aura about him which was quite indefinable. He had won his DSO bringing back just about half a plane from Cologne, and subsequently was awarded the DFC again whilst flying on 102 Squadron. These decorations generally came the other way round so one can only surmise what a feat of airmanship the Cologne trip had been. In his 617 days, his front gunner was none other than Wilf Bickley. Suffice to say, we had a very pleasant evening and to drink and chat with the greatest bomber pilot of all time was indeed a bonus.

Group Captain W. S. O. Randle CBE, AFC, DFM, FBIM

This is another post-war association, again the common denominator being Exmouth (my adopted home town).

Originally, I sent a sub to the Bomber Command Museum Appeal Fund and an acknowledgement came back from the above, containing the interesting fact that he was educated in Exmouth and was a contemporary of several of my friends. Further correspondence elicited the fact that as Director of the Museum he was a friend and colleague of Air Chief Marshal 'Gus' Walker, who incidentally also had Exmouth connections, as he used to spend some of his vacations as a Cambridge undergraduate in tutorial work in the town. Subsequent to our exchange of letters, a 'Forties Night' was held at the Beacon Vaults, Exmouth, thanks to the good office of the landlord, Bill Gatward, enabling us to make a contribution to the Museum Fund.

However, my appetite was whetted concerning Bill Randle's career and I discovered there were many facets. He trained in America and, as with many more aicrew, his ambition was to fly Spitfires. But this was not to be and he found himself operating Wellingtons over the Third Reich in 1942 and made twenty-seven operational trips before being shot down over Essen. With his crew he spent four months in enemy territory but eventually with the assistance of the Comet Line they returned home via Spain. These adventures alone would justify writing a book. But this experience did not mark the end of his operational flying. He took a conversion course and became an ace pilot on Mosquitoes which as he so rightly said, 'After so long on the Wellington, flying the Mossie was like comparing a rapier with a bludgeon.' He clocked up hundreds of hours on this aircraft and after the cessation of hostilities he flew a desk in the Intelligence section of Air Ministry. The early nineteen fifties heralded the Korean War and he was seconded to the United States Air Force. He saw more active service flying helicopters and in actual fact was the only RAF officer to fly operationally.

Not only was he a talented aviator but he became, because of his outstanding experiences, technical advisor to the BBC for their brilliant series of *Secret Army* and not the least of his achievements was to take the part of Oberleutnant Helmut Rath in the same production; the wheel had certainly turned full circle. He was also involved in other BBC productions and the more I learn of people of his calibre, the more I wonder at my own temerity in penning my inconsequential experiences.

Squadron Leader Richard Langworthy DFC, AFC

This was another post-war encounter as I met Richard and his distinguished twin brother when they were both Sergeants in the Air Training Corps at Exmouth. Their father was a good friend of mine and through him I met the boys who were flying mad. I used to shoot them the proverbial line, little thinking that their experiences would far outstrip mine. Richard served at Suez, Brunei, and Borneo, both in fighters and helicopters. He made an outstanding contribution in the Falklands campaign flying helicopters, and took off the only surviving RAF Chinook from the sinking *Atlantic Conveyor*. Group Captain Randle was his commanding officer at Odiham. Sadly, Richard died from natural causes on a second tour of the Falklands after the cessation of hostilities.

Wing Commander L. D. Wilson DSO, DFC, AFC

Most people's association with their commanding officer was normally limited to an interview after putting up some black. Fortunately, my contacts with the CO did not fall into this category, not that I was not guilty of my fair share of indiscretions. We did however mix socially on occasions as we both had our wives on the station at the same time.

As a leader, he conformed to his breed, he was to the manner born and what was paramount amongst a high spirited fraternity, he was a good mixer without forfeiting respect. I was not too happy when I knew he was on an op because they generally turned out to be sticky.

The story goes that one luckless pilot, in his hearing, tendered the view that you couldn't get a Halifax airborne on three engines with a full bomb load, an offer which to his chagrin was taken up by 'Willy'. I can't vouch for the authenticity of the story but it certainly had a typical ring. He finished his tour in early forty-five and was awarded a well earned DSO.

Sir Frederick Handley Page

The occasion of meeting Sir Frederick was when the last Halifax bomber *London Pride* was handed over to our crew on behalf of the Royal Air Force on the 16th April 1945. He was one of the giants of aviation history founding Handley Page Ltd in 1909. He was an enthusiastic advocate of the heavy bomber in which his interest went back to the First World War. At the request of the military hierarchy he built the very first four engine bomber, the V1500 which was the largest plane of World War I powered by four 375 horsepower Rolls Royce engines, mounted in pairs, a tractor and a pusher, it was capable of carrying three tons of bombs to Berlin. In actual fact, it was bombed up on November 11th, 1918 for that specific purpose but the Armistice was signed on that day so it was never operational in the war. Two other twin engine jobs, the 0/100 and 0/400 saw operational service and at the end of the war, there were two hundred and fifty-eight of the latter in operation.

Prior to the Second World War the Heyford was brought into service but, next to the Halifax, the most famous product of the stable was the Hampden, a twin engine bomber which first went into operation on September 4th 1939.

In all, 6,176 Halifaxes came off the production line, but apart from this aircraft perpetuating the manufacturer's name for all time, Sir Frederick himself is assured of his place in aviation history for the invention of the Handley Page Slot, an aerodynamic safety feature which first saw the light of day in 1920.

Handley Page Halifax

I make no apology for including the above under the heading of 'Personalities' because the aircraft became an integral part of the crew, our destinies were inexorably interdependent. The Halifax was christened in September 1940 by Lord Halifax with the words — "From Hull, Hell and Halifax, good Lord deliver us." It first saw operational service as early as March 1941 to become Britain's longest serving bomber.

As in the case of the Hurricane and the Spitfire, it suffered by comparison with the advent of the Lancaster and, although no one doubts the pedigree of the latter as the most successful bomber of the war, it could not match the versatility of the Halifax which operated in Europe, Italy, the Middle East, North Africa, the Far East, SOE and SAS operations, anti U-boat operations, and last but certainly not least, the towing of the Horsa and the huge Hamilcar in the operation 'Overlord'.

No other aircraft in World War II carried out such a diversity of operations:

> 'For when she flies on high, she's the Queen of the Sky,
> Is that old-fashioned Haly of mine.'

Not one single aircraft survived intact, a travesty and an oversight which can never be forgiven.

THE CREW — It seems rather strange, but looking back, despite the many hours we spent both in the air and on the ground, I knew very little of the personal lives of the crew. We were joined by a metaphorical umbilical cord because we all have one common denominator which nobody ever spoke about and that was fear.

Meyer, G. Lieutenant DFC

Gerry was our first pilot and at the time we were operating he was in the

South African Air Force, and like the rest wore the traditional khaki. He must have been a glutton for punishment as he had already completed a tour as an air gunner in the Middle East and sported the Africa Star. It never failed to amaze me that these colonials forsook their native shore and security to stick their necks out in what was basically our war. He was a very press-on type and the only difference of opinion we had was the night our fuel was running low and he still insisted on trying to find the target. He was a born flyer but I think he flew more by instinct than by the book. Without a doubt, he saved our lives one afternoon on take off which I have described earlier. If he had a fault, it was indigenous to all South Africans, you could be in their company and they would jabber away to each other in Afrikaans.

Bennett, M. B. Flight Lieutenant DFC and Bar

Maurice came as our second Skipper and was a real professional as far as the Halifax was concerned, having more hours in than I had hot dinners. He completed a tour when the going was really hard and was awarded the DFC. He was then seconded to 1664 Conversion Unit as an instructor and we passed through his hands at Dishforth. He was only twenty-two and a former bank clerk. I never saw him rattled and was an ice cold competitor who was well thought of at Group Headquarters. He was not the usual run of the mill aircrew and did not hit the high spots like the rest of the crew, which was probably a good job, he certainly might have had an equal but certainly not a superior when it came to handling a Halifax.

Berger, C. R. Pilot Officer

Colin was the bomb aimer for whom I had unlimited admiration. He was both big in stature and mind. He was a practising Jew and his chances of survival if we had been shot down were not remote, they were simply non-existent. He and I worked as a team, he assisted me with the navigation, holding on resolutely to Gee signals to the bitter end before the screen was swamped by Jerry jamming.

He gave us a fright one night when we were on the bombing run, he gave no response to the Skipper who was asking for course corrections and Gerry told me to see what the problem was. He had flaked out, the plug had disengaged from his oxygen point. I pushed it back in and lying on top of him, I tracked the target indicators coming down the illuminated graticule and pressed the tit to release nine one thousand pound bombs and four five hundreds.

He was another bod of complete integrity, no matter how much flak was coming up, he never shirked a target and hung on to the bitter end to ensure his bombs coincided with the target indicators. People of his calibre and faith were the salt of the earth.

Adlard, H. M. Pilot Officer

Harry was the rear gunner, a most phlegmatic Yorkshire character, I never ever saw him ruffled, call him up on the intercom and all you got out of him was, "OK Skipper." His was a long lonely vigil, nothing to do but scan the sky for five or six hours every trip; one advantage he had over other crew members, the only time he saw the target was when we had left it. He had a dry sense of humour and exerted a fatherly influence on some of us in our more boisterous moments.

Young, S. P. A. Sergeant

Steven was the engineer, which was a most onerous job involving the permutation of interchanging fuel on twelve tanks at different stages of an operation, his chief job was to ensure that there was a reserve of fuel in the event of an emergency. He was the youngest member of the crew and spent many an hour of which we were not aware tending his beloved engines. I am also sure that he believed we were indestructible. He was an ebullient character dedicated to his job although he had only just passed his eighteenth birthday.

Allen, D. A. Flight Sergeant

Was the mid upper gunner and quite convinced we were God's gift to Bomber Command which he extolled on the ground *ad nauseam* to anyone who would listen to him. He even thought I was a reincarnated Columbus, which I must say was very good for the ego. Over the target he was apt to put one off when he kept shouting — "There's a kite above you with his bomb doors open." This wasn't too good for crew morale as you were not exactly in a position to draw into the kerb. He was the life and soul of the party, and there certainly was never a dull moment when he was around. A great lad and a typical Scotsman.

Roach, L. M. Pilot Officer

Larry was the wireless operator, a New Zealander who looked old but looked forward to getting older, a sentiment I heartily shared. He didn't get me many fixes but with Gee and H2S wireless operators were almost surplus to requirements. But he certainly did a good job shovelling out window (metallic strips which were showered down by the main stream to blot out the enemy radar screens) a really boring but very necessary job. He never showed any signs of worry and I believe he used to relieve the ennui by tuning in to dance bands. He kept everybody on their toes on the deck. I always associated Larry with leave as he invariably gave a party piece on York Station singing 'Phil the Fluter's Ball' with all the physical manifestations, much to the amusement of fellow travellers. Fortunately there were some more New Zealanders on the squadron to keep him company and we were never at a loss for entertainment.

8

AIRBORNE POCKLINGTON

	Date	Target	Narrative	Day	Night
1944					
August	18th	CAEN	Diversion for Main Stream		3.30
	24th	BREST	Shipping & U-boat Pens	5.15	
September	1st	LA POURCHINTE	Doodle Bug Site	3.25	
	3rd	VENLO	Airfield	4.30	
	11th	NORDSTERN	Industrial & Oil	4.20	
October	6th	SCHOLVEN	Industrial & Oil	4.50	
	7th	KLEVE	Communications	4.30	
	14th	DUISBURG	Industrial	5.15	
	15th	WILHELMSHAVEN	Industrial & Shipping		4.25
	21st	HANOVER	Industrial (Recall)		2.15
	23rd	ESSEN	Industrial Attacked Munchen-Gladbeck		4.10
	30th	COLOGNE	Industrial		5.50
November	2nd	DUSSELDORF	Industrial		5.40
	6th	GELSENKIRCHEN	Oil	4.30	
	11th	FREDERIKSHAVN	Minelaying		5.45
	18th	MUNSTER	Industrial (Early Return)	1.20	
	30th	DUISBURG	Industrial & Docks		5.15
December	5th	SOEST	Marshalling Yards		6.30
	6th	OSNABRUCK	Communications		6.35
	21st	ARNHOLT	Minelaying		5.45
	24th	MULHEIM	Airfield Mulheim − Essen	5.00	
	29th	KOBLENZ	Communications		5.18

1945					
January	1st	DORTMUND	Railway Yards		4.45
	2nd	LUDWIGSHAFEN-MANNHEIM	Industrial		7.30
		Pilot Lt. G. Meyer. Screened & Awarded DFC			
February	1st	MAINZ	Railway Yards		6.40
	3rd	CUXHAVEN	Mining		4.55
	7th	GOCH	Communications		6.10
	13th	LEIPZIG	Industrial (Early Return)		2.30
	27th	MAINZ	Railway Yards	6.05	
March	2nd	COLOGNE	Industrial	5.20	
	3rd	KAMEN	Oil Plant		6.00
	5th	CHEMNITZ	Communications (Early Return)		1.20
	7th	FLENSBURG FIORD	Mining		5.30
	8th	HAMBURG	Mining		5.35
	13th	WUPPERTAL	Communications – Industrial	5.20	
	14th	HOMBURG	Communications – Industrial		5.50
	25th	OSNABRUCK	Communications – Industrial	5.20	
April	4th	HARBURG/ RHENANIA	Docks & Communications		5.15
	8th	HAMBURG	Docks & Communications		5.40
	10th	FLENSBURG FIORD	Mining		4.45

CREW SCREENED
Pilot
Flight Lieutenant M.B. Bennett, DFC
Awarded Bar to DFC

BIBLIOGRAPHY

Action Stations	Military Airfields of Yorkshire	Bruce Barrymore Halpenny, Patrick Stephens	1982
Aviation		Book Club Associates	1980
Aircraft Illustrated	(October 1979)	Ian Allen	
Bomber Command	Max Hastings	Michael Joseph	1979
Daily Telegraph			
Enemy Coast Ahead	Guy Gibson	Michael Joseph	1946
Famous Bombers of the Second World War	William Green	Book Club Associates	1979
Collins Gem Gazetteer of the World		William Collins	1973
New Shell Guide to England		Book Club Associates	1981
Night Pilot	Jean Calmel	William Kimber	1955
Pears Cyclopaedia		Book Club Associates	1981
Raider	Geoffrey Jones	William Kimber	1978
Royal Air Force		Book Club Associates	1981
Terror By Night	Michael Renaut	William Kimber	1982
The Bomber		Birmingham Post and Mail	1982
The Role of the Bomber	Ronald W. Clark	Sidgwick and Jackson	1977
White Rose Base	Brian J. Rapier	Aero Litho	1972
World Aircraft		Sampson Low	1978